Praise for *STAND FIRM* an

'An exhilarating broadside against the intense modern pressure to do more, be more, to become happier and more productive, and to "find yourself". In championing Stoicism over the relentless and exhausting wild-goose chase of self-help, Svend Brinkmann – though he might not like the fact – has written a book that truly helps.'
Oliver Burkeman, columnist, *The Guardian*

'A bracing and defiant manifesto.'
The Sydney Morning Herald

'This wonderfully funny and intelligent book not only exposes the foolishness of the self-help cult, but also offers a concrete and appealing alternative, reminding us that philosophy is as relevant for living our lives today as it has ever been.'
Carl Cederström, Stockholm Business School

'Every once in a while a book comes along that is both ironic and serious, both funny and challenging, both timely and wise. *Stand Firm*, with its seven steps toward living against our accelerated culture of "self-realisation", is such a book. It should be on the bookshelf of every person concerned with the state of the world – or with the state of themselves.'
Todd May, Clemson University

The Joy of Missing Out

Svend Brinkmann

THE JOY OF MISSING OUT

The Art of Self-Restraint in an Age of Excess

Translated by Tam McTurk

polity

First published in Danish as Gå glip © Gyldendal, 2017
Reprinted: 2019 (five times), 2020

This English edition © Polity Press, 2019

Polity Press
65 Bridge Street
Cambridge CB2 1UR, UKw

Polity Press
101 Station Landing
Suite 300
Medford, MA 02155, USA

ISBN-13: 978-1-5095-3156-1
ISBN-13: 978-1-5095-3157-8(pb)

A catalogue record for this book is available from the British Library.

Library of Congress Cataloging-in-Publication Data

Names: Brinkmann, Svend, author.
Title: The joy of missing out : the art of self-restraint in an age of excess
  / Svend Brinkmann.
Description: Cambridge, UK ; Medford, MA : Polity Press, [2019] | Includes
  bibliographical references and index.
Identifiers: LCCN 2018032456 (print) | LCCN 2018035333 (ebook) | ISBN
  9781509531592 (Epub) | ISBN 9781509531561 (hardback) | ISBN
9781509531578
  (pbk.)
Subjects: LCSH: Moderation. | Self-control. | Consumption (Economics)--Social
  aspects. | Excess (Philosophy)
Classification: LCC BJ1533.M7 (ebook) | LCC BJ1533.M7 B75 2019 (print) | DDC
  179/.9--dc23
LC record available at https://lccn.loc.gov/2018032456

Typeset in 11 on 14 pt Sabon by
Servis Filmsetting Ltd, Stockport, Cheshire
Printed and bound in the United Sates by LSC Communications

For further information on Polity, visit our website: politybooks.com

Contents

Aus Mäßigkeit entspringt ein reines Glück.
(True happiness springs from moderation.)

Johann Wolfgang von Goethe,
The Natural Daughter, 1803

Preface

This book is all about the art of self-restraint and the value of missing out. In it, I argue that, on a collective level, it is absolutely imperative for all nations, but especially the richest ones, to master this art if we are to make a better job of addressing the crises of the present and of the future. I also contend that, on a personal level, it is valuable *per se* for individuals to learn the art of 'making do' rather than wanting everything, here and now. The book makes a virtue out of necessity, mounting a passionate defence of what some might consider old-fashioned thinking about how we live our lives. It also has more of a political dimension than its predecessors, *Stand Firm* and *Standpoints*, even though it still focuses on the basic ethical and existential themes with which people appear to be increasingly preoccupied these days. While *Stand Firm* criticised the self-development mania, *Standpoints* sought to identify the basic ethical values upon which it is worth standing firm. In *The Joy of Missing Out*, I discuss ways of living our lives that would make it possible for society as a whole to focus on these values. As such, it works well with its predecessors. To *stand firm* on one thing, you must necessarily *miss out* on another. We may not find that easy, but it is nevertheless an existential, ethical and psychological necessity.

As well as a huge thanks to Anne Weinkouff, I would like to thank Anders Petersen, Lene Tanggaard, Ester Holte Kofod, Thomas Aastrup Rømer and Thomas Szulevicz, all of whom have given so generously of their time, reading the manuscript and making valuable comments that informed the final version. I would also like to thank Tam McTurk for his, as ever, excellent translation into English, and finally the whole team at Polity for helping to bring my work to an international audience.

Introduction:
Having It All

'Because you're worth it', proclaims the classic cosmetics ad. 'Just do it!' implores the world-famous sporting goods company. At every turn, we are spurred on to experience as *much* as possible, for as *long* as possible, in as *many* contexts as possible. Thankfully, we are under no compulsion to actually comply, but there is no doubt that these slogans reflect a culture that has long cultivated the idea of 'as much as possible, as quickly as possible'. And why not? Why hold back when we have the choice? For reasons of time and money? On the cusp of the 1990s, the rock group Queen sang 'I want it all, and I want it now', a eulogy to *wanting more* that has served as a leitmotif in modern culture ever since.

Life is short – tragically so, in Freddie Mercury's case – so we have to see, do and experience as much as possible *now*, before it is too late. No compromise! Or so many people think. 'Having it all' has become an ideal, and we must all rush around seizing the day. *Carpe diem* is one of the most common tattoos, and the acronym *YOLO* (You Only Live Once) is in widespread (mis)use on social media. We tell each other that it is preferable to

1

do something we might regret than to regret not doing it. Missing out on something is the worst-case scenario. We live with *FOMO* (Fear of Missing Out) – another popular acronym – and are forever checking our phones for status updates, football scores, special deals or whatever happens to be our cup of tea. But doing it all is not easy, and so we need help. On Amazon, a search for 'get more done' comes up with more than 2,000 books, e.g. *Get More Done in Less Time – And Get On With the Good Stuff*. A simpler search on 'do more' comes up with more than 13,000 hits, from *Do More Better: A Practical Guide to Productivity* to *Do More in Less Time: How You Can Achieve Your Goals and Live a Balanced Life*. What you will not find are many books about doing less – let alone how to do less and take longer over it. But in a stressful age, is that not perhaps exactly what we need to learn?

The question is how to maintain focus in a world full of choice and temptation. We are constantly bombarded with invitations, in the broadest sense of the word, via everything from street advertising to social media. We are constantly invited to do something, think something, experience something, buy something, consume something. Competition for our attention spans is fierce, and when inundated by overwhelming amounts of information it is sometimes difficult to distinguish what is important from what is not. We try to 'surf the net' (as they said in the 1990s), this humungous wave of information, but often end up wiping out and struggling to keep our heads above water. Much of our life is now spent training ourselves, in one way or another, to experience as much as possible. We are tempted by quick loans, special offers and just one more episode of our favourite TV series, courtesy of on-demand stream-ing services. As a species, we have created a society with a cultural landscape, an ecological niche, based on invi-tations, temptations, choices and special offers, but we rarely practise the art of self-restraint, of saying no and opting out – those are skills we lack both as individu-als and as a society. This book recommends making a virtue of necessity and practising the art of missing out.

Learning these skills has become a necessity because for so long our lives have been based on overconsump-tion, untrammelled growth and whittling away at our natural resources. That is the theme of the next chapter. We can and should discuss the precise details of the crises that humanity has provoked, and which frame our existence, but it is a matter of documented, scien-tific *fact* that these self-inflicted crises *do* exist, and that is one of the foundations on which this book is based. The virtue to which necessity must and will lead us is not some hippy-dippy eco-utopia, but one of the main pillars in a philosophical tradition stretching back to ancient Greece, when moderation was considered an essential character trait. In those days, moderation (*sophrosyne* in Greek) was often heralded as one of the cardinal virtues – in other words, a necessary component of any kind of ethical activity. According to the ancient Greeks, it is only possible to embody other virtues, such as courage and generosity, if we exercise moderation in everything we do – if we master the art of missing out. If we 'want it all', then being good at something specific, including in the ethical sense, will elude us. According to this way of thinking, living a full, rich and flourish-ing life requires a degree of self-mastery and self-control – not as a form of masochistic self-flagellation or as an ascetic or anorexic project, in which saying no has a value *per se*, but as a prerequisite for our ability to do our best, as the individuals we happen to be, with the responsibilities we happen to have, in the contexts we happen to find ourselves.

When modern psychology discusses moderation and temperance, it is usually in the context of exercising self-control. While such approaches are significant, in this book the psychological aspect of missing out on something is considered to be only one of several relevant dimensions. I have identified five of them and present them here as overarching arguments in the five chapters to follow.

I start with a chapter on the *political argument*, which is all about our collective life, and outlines the basic justification for learning to make do. The planet has limited resources but its population continues to grow, and recent decades have seen an upsurge in inequality in many countries. If we want life to be sustainable for the maximum possible number of people – ideally, for all of us – then we need to learn the art of self-restraint, especially here in the richest part of the world.

Next, I introduce the *existential argument*. In Søren Kierkegaard's somewhat pompous turn of phrase, opting out and maintaining focus are all about being pure of heart: 'Purity of heart is to will one thing.' Existential reflection must entail an acknowledgement that we should not want it all (as the poet Piet Hein suggested); rather, we must pay attention to something specific in order for our lives to be lived well and not just be some kind of amorphous blur.

I then proceed to the *ethical argument*, which is about our relationship to others, the basic idea being that we are only able to live up to our obligations as human beings if we are willing to miss out on something in order to be there for other, specific, people. It is here in particular that the classic idea of virtue becomes relevant, with its concept of moderation (*sophrosyne*) as a key component of an ethical life.

The next argument is the *psychological* one, which in tangible terms is about practising self-control, and why this is difficult amidst the myriad temptations of the experience-obsessed consumer society. The human psyche appears to have a tragic aspect, sometimes dubbed the 'hedonic treadmill'. Once we have achieved something for which we have strived, we grow accustomed to it and the attraction soon wears off. We then come up with something else to strive for, in a never-ending pursuit of happiness that only stops when we die. The more we have, the more we want. On the face of it, it seems strange that even people in our part of the world, which in historical terms is incredibly rich, work themselves half to death, or worse, in order to earn more. Can we break this vicious circle?

The final argument in favour of missing out is derived from *aesthetics*. The idea of beauty in simplicity is a classic one, found in both art and science. Perhaps it also applies to the art of living? I argue that there is aesthetic value in simple rituals that organise our daily lives and free up energy and resources for more significant activities. The chapter also attempts to suggest more specific ways in which we can practise the art of self-restraint. Making a virtue out of necessity can become a life art.

Taken together, these five arguments show that not only is there a political imperative to the art of self-restraint, there is also an existential depth, an ethical potential, a psychological benefit and an aesthetic quality to missing out. Dividing the discussion up into these different domains is not the only way to address the issue, and there are no rigid boundaries between (for example) the existential domain and psychology, or politics and ethics. The chapters overlap, but can also be read on their own. I labour under no misapprehension that readers will agree with all five arguments, but my hope is that they will still get something out of reading the book. Some may focus on the psychological dimension and reject the political – others will see it the other way round. My own goal is to draw on analyses of the many different aspects of life to show that missing out has greater fundamental value than most people might think. We can all learn to focus, to opt out, to settle for less of that which is actually trivial – and then hopefully have more time for what is significant. The anthropologist Harry Wolcott used to advise his PhD students to 'Do less, more thoroughly.'[1] Perhaps more of us should heed his advice – not just in our studies, but throughout our lives. To do so, we must have the courage to commit to something and to miss out more.

1

The Sustainable Society

The first book I helped edit as a budding young researcher critiqued the demand for personal development and its tendency to spill over into more and more aspects of life. This has remained a leitmotif in much of my subsequent work: the fact that we live in a rampant *development culture* that knows no *boundaries*. It is a culture that manifests itself in the countless demands for flexibility, adaptability and willingness to change that we encounter at work and in our educational institutions.[1] A great deal more (critical) attention has been paid to this dimension in recent times, but the boundless aspect is also worth noting – the fact that it has become difficult ever to say that someone or something is *good enough*. We are all supposed to be engaged in lifelong learning processes, i.e. processes with no end. They never stop. Nobody can ever tell the boss at a performance review that they have reached the pinnacle of professional development. Political reforms never cease either, nor do they ever reach a final, finished form. In the 1990s, Philip Cerny introduced the concept of the competition state to describe the way that modern nations operate in a globalised market, and essentially think of themselves as businesses. In his book on the competitive state, Ove Kaj Pedersen talks of 'never-ending reforms', describing how the public sector has developed since the 1970s, with constant rounds of reorganisation of the state, its functions and its staffing needs.[2] Just think of the recent reforms of schools, universities, social security, etc., in many Western countries. The demands for skills enhancement and optimisation are constant and never-ending, which logically leads to a situation where nobody ever does anything well enough, because we all know that we will soon be instructed to do more and do it better. Everything is monitored, quantified and evaluated to facilitate 'visible learning' in education and at work. In our 'learning organisations', all progress has to be visible to inspire everybody to do 'even better'.

On the one hand, it is a culture that knows no boundaries in the sense that its demands can never be met – the goalposts move every time you approach the penalty box. On the other hand, it also knows no boundaries in the sense that we are called upon to develop and optimise in absolutely every area of our lives. Workplaces demand not just professional but also personal development. Children are expected to perform well in the classroom, but also to be healthy, creative, musical and good at sports. This lack of boundaries is not only reflected in the purely temporal aspect of life (historians call this the *diachronic* dimension), but also transcends multiple areas of life at any given time (the *synchronic* dimension). We live in a rampant development culture with no brakes, nothing holding it back. Not only does this jeopardise our individual well-being (which was one of the themes of *Stand Firm*), but it is also unsustainable at an overarching level.

There is no doubt that humanity urgently needs to discuss sustainability and to make changes to many aspects of consumer society, but many people are already tired of the concept. I know the feeling. One day, I caught myself saying, 'Isn't sustainability just a buzzword that we tag onto everything without it really meaning anything?' Sometimes. But in its simplest form, sustainability just means living in a way that does not squander and deplete natural resources. It means ensuring that the world we pass on to the next generation is in at least as good a condition as we found it. This is not some outlandish hippy ideal – it should be common sense. But are human beings actually capable of building a sustainable society? Is it already too late? Many scientists believe that we now live in a geological epoch called the *Anthropocene* (from the Greek *antropos*, meaning man), which refers to the fact that human impact on the planet is on a par with tectonic plate movements or volcanic eruptions. Humankind has become a force of nature – with global and devastating consequences.

A 2011 article that introduced the concept of the Anthropocene epoch to the Danish public explained that industrial society uses four or five times as much energy as previous agricultural communities, which in turn used three or four times as much energy as the previous hunter-gatherer cultures.[3] The population of the world has risen from around 1 billion in 1800 to around 7.5 billion now. During the same period, energy consumption has risen forty-fold and production fifty-fold. The consequences are all too apparent, with greater CO_2 concentration in the atmosphere, higher temperatures and more extreme weather events. The number of people who have been displaced by climate change (climate refugees) is already twice as high as the number fleeing from war, even though wars are not exactly in short supply. Human activity is also having a detrimental effect on biodiversity, with almost two-thirds of animal species dying out in the last forty-five years or so.[4] Sustainability may well have become a bit of a buzzword, but with good reason. There is no shortage of scientists pessimistically asserting that it is already too late, that the planet has passed its tipping point, that we cannot save it from climate change and we face the prospect of multiple horrific catastrophes in the not-too-distant future.[5] Will that be the ultimate consequence of our rampant development culture?

It is probably too early to tell, but it certainly looks as if this alarmist, fear-inducing rhetoric has failed to persuade sufficient numbers of people to embrace sustainability. Concerned scientists are sometimes dismissed as attention-seeking doom merchants with a need for renewed funding for their research. Some reactions border on the apathetic – if it is too late, then we might as well enjoy life as much as possible for as long as possible. It is an attitude reminiscent of the *Titanic* – as the water flooded into the ship the orchestra played on, and people kept dancing and drinking until they drowned. However, my mission with this book is not to ratchet up the fear factor. I simply wish to present the concept of a modest, sustainable life within certain boundaries as an attractive alternative for individuals and society alike. As a way of life, it has a certain elementary dignity to it. As previously mentioned, it looks as if it will be imperative to break with the 'more, more, more' thinking that has held sway for centuries, but which critical voices have always challenged. Using ethical or psychological language, these voices have often claimed that failure to master the art of self-restraint is tantamount to inflicting self-harm. They have now been joined by other voices putting forward environmental and geopolitical arguments for a more sustainable society.

Climate change has not been the only cause of global crises in recent years. Many also believe that a runaway, unregulated form of capitalism has led to a problematic level of inequality and widespread fear, discontent and conflict around the globe. However, the good news is that the number of people living in absolute poverty has been falling steadily in recent decades. Many people are better off and better educated these days, and infant mortality has been reduced. Unfortunately, the other side of this coin is that the inequality gap has widened in many countries – it is now a well-known fact that the richest 1 per cent of the world's population owns more than the rest of us put together, and that the eight richest individuals own as much as the poorest half of the world's population.[6] It is not just between countries that the differences in economic prosperity have been exacerbated, but also within many of them. Social scientists of different political persuasions have discussed the consequences of this surge in inequality at great length, but the evidence suggests that greater inequality is statistically associated with more disease and crime and less social mobility and innovation – at least in the OECD countries studied by Wilkinson and Pickett for their controversial book *The Spirit Level*.[7] One of the main points they make is that economic equality is good for everyone. When society is relatively equal, life improves for the most affluent too – they live longer, healthier lives, experience less stress, etc. A society that is sustainable, including in terms of economic equality, is a society in which all social groups feel they are doing well. Of course, this does not mean that it is desirable for everybody to own and consume exactly the same amounts. Only a totalitarian ideology would seek to impose a nightmarish scenario in which people lack the freedom to influence their own level of prosperity. But it does suggest that growing inequality needs to be taken seriously as a causal factor behind several societal problems. Analysts generally agree on this. For example, José Ángel Gurría, Secretary General of the OECD, recently warned that we have reached a 'tipping point' with regard to galloping inequality, and that the situation is analogous to climate change.[8] Once both inequality and rising temperatures reach a certain point, it is difficult – if not impossible – to change course, because numerous self-perpetuating effects come into play. Even the OECD now accepts that greater equality would benefit everyone – including the richest.

What has caused the climate crisis and growing inequality? The answers lie in a combination of factors – it is not possible to identify a single engine of historical change that has triggered them. It is easy to point the finger at capitalism, but that is actually a rather general term that encompasses multiple social models. It would also be fair to say that attempts to overthrow capitalism and replace it with a different system have, in many cases, proven worse than the social disease they sought to cure (think of the Soviet Union, where revolution led to a totalitarian regime ruled by a narrow party elite). Capitalism has framed our way of thinking and acting for so long that it is hard to step out of the box and evaluate it objectively. Do we just have to live with it as it is? Possibly, but perhaps change has been afoot in recent years. According to Karl Marx, the development of technology played a major historical role in the development of society per se. The journalist Paul Mason, in his bestseller *Postcapitalism*,[9] writes about how the capitalist system as we know it is being undermined by the very advances in technology that have driven the economy in the past. He argues that, in the first place, new (digital) technology reduces the demand for labour, as manifest in growing robotisation and automation, a process still in its infancy. Secondly, it leads to an abundance of non-material goods that make it difficult for the market to regulate prices. Traditionally, market mechanisms have been based on scarcity of resources, but the digital world is awash with information, music, literature, etc. Thirdly, we are witnessing the rise of collaborative forms of production (sometimes described by buzzwords like 'the sharing economy') that sometimes outperform established industries, e.g. Wikipedia, which has rendered traditional encyclopaedias all but obsolete.[10]

However, the question is whether social acceleration really is a significant historical force driving both capitalism and post-capitalism, assuming the latter exists or ever will. The sociologist Hartmut Rosa would say so and has devised a whole new theory of modernity based on an analysis of social acceleration.[11] In brief, the theory goes that more or less everything – social processes and all sorts of human activities – has a tendency to speed up without any concomitant increase in leisure time. We then need to keep developing new technologies and practices to help us get more done, and the spiral accelerates. This has been the case at least since the Industrial Revolution. The problem, as discussed earlier, is that modern society is based on a linear conception of *more, more, more* – or 'harder, better, faster, stronger', as Daft Punk's robotic voice intones in their smash hit of the same name – and lacks checks and balances. The type of cultural baggage that had a restraining effect during the industrial area – which valued moderation and delayed gratification, for example – has all but disappeared.

From the industrial era to the rise of the knowledge or consumer society, societies have changed enormously not just in terms of their underlying economics but also, and just as much, in terms of mentality. The sociologist Zygmunt Bauman described this in many of his books as the transition from a solid culture epitomised by savings books, with an emphasis on thrift and delayed gratification, to a credit card culture that encourages people to 'pursue their dreams' and consume at rates they cannot afford. Bauman described consumer society's modernity as 'liquid', so the individual has to be liquid in order to keep up.[12] This is the crux of the matter and the challenge facing humankind – how do you argue against the ideals of having, doing, experiencing and consuming more?[13] After all, these are the very things that generate growth and keep the wheels turning, as politicians like to put it. The good citizen has become the good consumer who is never satisfied with what he or she has. Once, the good citizen was parsimonious, conscientious and acknowledged the value of self-restraint. Nowadays, the good citizen is all-consuming, knows no boundaries and never stops striving to get ahead. If you are satisfied, there is no incentive to acquire more

– which, in a consumer society and economy based on us constantly wanting more, makes satisfaction a vice rather than a virtue. Anxiety about status has become commonplace, an all-too familiar feeling in a society built on performance: Am I good enough? What do others think of me?[14] By contrast, this book highlights the benefits of being content – the message being that you have nothing to fear, as opting out and missing out will help you appreciate what you have.

I would contend that coping with real-world challenges, such as climate change and massive global inequality, requires a greater willingness to be satisfied with what we have. We must learn to 'make do' and sometimes miss out. Otherwise, it is difficult to imagine that a sustainable society – in tune with nature, in which people work together harmoniously and where the equality gap is not too large – would ever be feasible.

But is that not a somewhat condescending and hypocritical message when conveyed by a relatively wealthy person living in one of the richest and safest parts of the world? Is it not a distinctly elitist and privileged attitude to believe that we must learn to 'make do'? That is all very well for those who want for nothing! It is important to address this legitimate objection before we proceed any further.

The elitist trap

The elitist trap refers to a situation in which the wealthy and privileged use arguments about the (perceived) need for savings or cuts to keep others down. This is the trap that people risk falling into when, for example, they reproach others for not eating organic food or for filling their children with artificial additives. The problem is, of course, that it takes resources – both financial and psychological – to familiarise yourself with these issues and shop in the 'right' way. The affluent can afford to buy organic, but it is far more difficult for families with little money or those who lack the time to read books about the Stone Age Diet and optimum nutrition. Organic free-range chickens are, quite simply, far more expensive than battery-raised ones. A similar problem exists between countries. A well-off country like Denmark may well be able to meet targets for CO_2 reductions (or should be able to, at least) by outsourcing production to other countries and trading in CO_2 quotas. It is all very well for us to talk about a simple, frugal life when we are enormously wealthy. Developing economies, which still struggle to reach the standard of living we have enjoyed for many decades, do not want to be told to cut back, lower their ambitions for material wealth or emit less CO_2.

In terms of the structure of this book, this chapter on politics comes before the existential, ethical, psychological and aesthetic chapters because, if we are to avoid the elitist trap, it is important to think in political terms, which in this context means much more than just party politics. The concept of politics stems from the Greek word for city, *polis*, and is used here in its original meaning of 'things pertaining to collective life'. In other words, decisions that affect all members of a group are, in a fundamental sense, necessarily political. While the following chapters deal with how individuals can find meaning in missing out, the point of this chapter is that the debate must also take place at the collective level, because that is where the crucial decisions are made. If, for example, we want everybody in the country to be able to afford organic chicken now and again, a political choice could be made to impose price limits on organic food. If we want to cut CO_2 emissions, we could introduce taxes on fuel to restrict consumption. If our democratically elected representatives believe that a high degree of equality is a worthy goal, then progressive taxation could be the order of the day. Most people would probably prefer these solutions to, for example, leaving it up to wealthy people to pay more taxes if they want to, or asking the individual 'political consumer' to cut down on cheap flights.

Similarly, the sustainability debate ought to be based on political discussions about the direction in which we would like to see society head, as well as how much abuse nature and the environment can take. Of course it is a good thing if individuals voluntarily sort their rubbish, but it undeniably works best and most effectively if measures are introduced at a collective level – and indeed, under democratic control, so that voters exert an influence on the recycling system. Social problems ought to be solved politically, not privatised down to the individual level; nor should people's private problems be subject to government intervention (indeed, how to distinguish between collective political matters and individual ones is an important political debate). This is also where the discussions about sustainability and inequality are interrelated, because in highly unequal societies the solutions to collective problems are increasingly being outsourced to individuals. We talk about the individualisation of social problems, for example when the individual – despite high national unemployment rates – is accused of lacking the motivation to find a job. This may be a factor, but the bigger problem is more likely the structural shortage of jobs, in which case it is unfair to make the individual find 'biographical solutions' to 'systemic contradictions', as the sociologist Ulrich Beck put it in his critique of individualisation.[15] Beck was the originator of the theory of the risk society, which he defined as our attempt to deal with the uncertainties generated by modern society itself. Of course, life has always been uncertain and risky, and humankind has had to respond collectively to earthquakes, floods, droughts, etc. But, suddenly, with modernity and all of its consequences – industrialisation, technology, urbanisation and rationalisation – the primary risks (pollution, overpopulation, climate change, etc.) now stem from society's own behaviour. The main threats to humankind were once posed by the forces of nature; now they are self-inflicted, we are the cause of our own problems, and they can only be solved at the level of the society that created them. In the Anthropocene epoch, new technologies have created new problems and risks, which – almost paradoxically – we are now seeking to address by developing yet more new technology. It remains to be seen whether we will succeed in creating a new 'green technology' capable of solving the problems created by the older wasteful variety, but in the meantime it is crucial that we do more than just passively hope that our future technology will save us. One helpful step would be to collectively rediscover the ancient virtues of frugality, moderation and the art of missing out as means of counteracting social acceleration and its damaging effects.

The Sustainable Society

Getting less than your due

In the following chapters, I study and recommend the value of accepting less than we are due. For the modern individual who thinks in terms of optimisation and cost-benefit analysis, this is almost sacrilege. Is life not all about 'making the most of it', and getting as much as possible in as many different contexts as possible? Not necessarily. Not only in our everyday lives, but also in political contexts, there may be good reason to settle for less than we think we deserve. In a thought-provoking book called *On Settling*, the political philosopher Robert Goodin refers to research by historians and political scientists showing that after a conflict between countries or groups (including after wars), a durable peace is more likely if the victorious party accepts less than it might have received. The most obvious warning from history is the behaviour of the victors after the First World War and the massive reparations demanded from the defeated Germans.[16] Although the historical significance of this revenge exacted on Germany is a matter of some debate (counterfactual history writing is notoriously difficult), there is strong evidence to suggest that the problems it triggered in the country helped to pave the way for Hitler and the Nazis – and thus indirectly for the Second World War and the manmade disasters it inflicted. Shortly after the Great War, the economist John Maynard Keynes warned that reparations would lead to a 'Carthaginian peace', referring to the Romans' merciless treatment of Carthage after the Second Punic War. If we want to learn from history, it is worth considering what might have happened had the victors been less greedy after their victory in 1918.

Making do with less than you could have obtained is a form of magnanimity that the ancient philosophers called *meionexia*. According to most political thinkers, the normative objective after a war would not be blind revenge, but *jus post bellum* (a just end to war). *Meionexia* is key.[17] One aspect of this virtue is that it requires a mature and well-cultivated mind to settle for less than might have been. It is difficult to miss out on something desirable if it is within your grasp. According to the political scientist Benjamin Barber, who excoriates consumer society in his book *Consumed*, the requisite intellectual maturity is in short supply these days.[18] Barber believes that consumer society renders us childish. Remember the advertising slogans at the start of this book, exhorting us to want it all – and want it now! Barber shows how capitalism used to revolve around producing goods and commodities, with a focus on efficiency and reliability, whereas modern consumer capitalism generates needs and desires. Of course, people have always had needs, but the economy used to strive to meet them, whereas the emphasis now is on creating new needs. Many companies have advertising budgets that exceed the costs of manufacturing their products – the whole machinery of society is very much geared to engender dissatisfaction with what you have (because it is not the newest or smartest) and an almost unbridled lust for something more and something else. Most of us know this. It does not take long for my brand-new car, which I have long coveted to the point of obsession, to become the 'new normal', and I find myself wanting a different one. This embarrassing and allegedly childish behaviour is suddenly desirable. Once a vice, it is now a virtue. Like kids, we are supposed to 'want it all'. I think we do children a disservice in using the term childish here. Evidence suggests that they are actually generous and have a strong sense of what is fair and just.

Not-so-simple living

This trend toward an unbridled consumer mentality with respect to both material goods and perhaps also to human relationships has, of course, been criticised over the years, and various alternatives have emerged. About ten to fifteen years ago, the lifestyle concept of 'simple living' was quite popular, and bestsellers about the phenomenon were published in multiple languages. Simple living became an actual movement, but when I Google the term now, most of the hits link to websites about exquisite Scandinavian furniture and interior design. Judging from the pictures, living simply is really expensive! Why did simple living have such a short shelf-life? Perhaps because it mainly targeted the affluent and resourceful, those who were able to live simply and nicely, who had the time to meditate and find inner peace. For most people, this is not a real option. They have bills to pay and packed lunches to prepare.[19]

In his analysis of the 'simple living' movement, the philosopher Jerome Segal concludes that it was simply too individualistic, and quickly degenerated into mere self-help.[20] He does not think that this detracts from the positive kernel in its ideas, but argues that it was a 'how' movement, i.e. it offered a means to happiness for the privileged, but contained no social dimension or in-depth consideration of underlying values. It became, as it were, a philosophy of life without any philosophical

21

content. In his own book, *Graceful Simplicity*, Segal (who, interestingly, used to work for the United States House Committee on the Budget) tried to outline an economic and political basis for a simpler and more sustainable life. In his opinion, this would involve confronting contemporary economic thinking by turning to Aristotle, who a couple of millennia ago asked the very fundamental question: what is the purpose of the economy? Segal and Aristotle both answer that the purpose of the economy is not to provide us with more and more, but to liberate us financially to live the good life. It is pointless, therefore, to discuss the economy without any conception of what constitutes the good life. Many economists would contend that the good life consists in the realisation of individual wishes and preferences – whatever they may be. Segal thinks, *à la* Aristotle, that it is possible to discuss the legitimacy of our preferences in a rational manner, not least in the light of ethical values. Most of us have some preferences that are not particularly desirable, because they are either immoral or not very sustainable. A lot of people want to be as rich as possible, but Aristotle believed that money can quickly become too much of a good thing and distract people from what is truly important in life. Later advocates of simplicity, like the nineteenth-century philosopher Henry David Thoreau, also noted that people need very little to live well, but still submit themselves to endless toil.

As well as discussing a number of specific proposals for a simpler life, Segal believes that one way of progressing away from the consumer society is to make the inherent value of work the focal point of the economy. It is often said that if we are engaged in something meaningful, work is almost its own reward – suggesting that it is from the qualitative content of our work that we should seek to derive satisfaction. However, many people feel they do not have a meaningful job. In a 2015 British study, 37 per cent of respondents stated that their work *does not* contribute meaningfully to the world.[21] Conversely, 50 per cent thought that their work was meaningful. It is not hard to imagine how easy it would be to become alienated from your work if you found it meaningless – or worse, if you thought the world would be a better place if your job ceased to exist.

The anarchist anthropologist David Graeber argues that the world is full of 'bullshit jobs' that serve no useful social function.[22] In a bullshit job, qualitative value is of no concern. All that matters is the quantitative aspect – how high is the salary? However, if we are able to identify what has inherent meaning in life, then it becomes easier to focus on this and ignore that which is devoid of meaning.[23] The problem is that we seldom have the opportunity to even consider this question, since it requires time for discussion and reflection. The last few decades of management thinking, driven by the notions of *new public management* and *lean production*, can be criticised for having diverted attention from the qualitative content of work activities in favour of a focus on 'how much', 'how fast', 'for how long' and 'getting more bang for our buck'.

According to Segal, reflection on meaningfulness also depends on leisure time. He celebrates leisure as an art form that we can learn – one that requires a special kind of discipline. Leisure is not necessarily aimless, but includes engaging in ritualised habits and practices in the company of others. For example, Segal, who is

Jewish, advocates the importance of the Sabbath as an organised, disciplined form of leisure in a communal setting. Ritualised interaction creates a collective focus and provides a refuge in which it is legitimate for people to relax and perhaps reflect on questions other than those that occupy them during their working lives. This can be done under the auspices of religious communities, in community centres, in adult education, but also in day-to-day interaction, during which family members talk about their day. In the final chapter of the book, I argue that ritualised practices are important because they provide a framework for our lives and a focus for our attention – often in an aesthetic way – that makes it easier for us to miss out on all the insignificant things.

Miss out on what?

I am not claiming for a moment that my brief overview of these very complex issues in any way constitutes an in-depth analysis of the unsustainability of consumer society, its lack of limits and its mechanisms that engender inequality. The sole intention has been to outline historical and political developments in order to underpin the following existential, ethical, psychological and aesthetic discussions of the art of self-restraint, and to introduce the concept of the necessity of missing out as being no great hardship, but as something positively beneficial.

As implied earlier, in a sense this was also the point of the simple living movement, only it turned out to be too elitist and individualistic and failed to define what precisely was to be ditched. It turned out that living simply is anything but simple, because in order to do so, the individual must possess quite substantial resources. If we want a collective debate about what we should miss out on as a society, we need to use our democratic institutions. We need to understand that, in order to live our individual lives, each of us relies on the collective. The difference between the individual and society should not be posited as a dichotomy, since the two are basically interdependent. A welfare state like Denmark is probably better positioned than many other countries to ensure the provision of essential goods in a way that means individuals are not doomed to strive eternally for *more, more, more.* As Segal says in his book, it is advantageous for a society to build healthy and beautiful cities, since the people who live in them do not have to earn as much in order to share in their benefits. People who live in communities with good public parks and squares find it less necessary to have their own garden; if society provides good libraries, museums and decent public transport, we are close to the basis for a way of life in which Aristotle would have thrived. Indeed, all of this could be achieved without the subjugation of women and slaves that, in Aristotle's day, enabled free male citizens to enjoy a life spent in collective philosophical discussion. Segal mentions reading good books as a symbol of a life of simplicity. For him, the joy of literature is the greatest gift you can give your children. I agree, but would add that other valuable phenomena and activities can supplement books or fulfil the same function as them. The point about books though is that it can be free to read them and a decent education is needed in order to appreciate them properly. Similarly, a good education is essential if we want our children to learn the art of missing out – it is not something that we just master automatically.

This brings us to the crucial dilemma behind the political argument for learning to make do: if we start to decide for others what they should miss out on, does this not run counter to the spirit of liberal democracy? Shouldn't everybody be free to decide this for themselves? I would contend that such freedom *is* a fundamental value, but these days it conflicts with a legitimate desire to resolve the crises discussed in this chapter. On the one hand, we should not sacrifice individual liberty on the altar of a nanny state, but on the other hand we need to acknowledge that freedom cannot simply be defined negatively – as freedom *from* other people's interference. It must also be understood positively, as the freedom to read, write, calculate, reason, participate in democracy and take responsibility for our own lives, as well as the life of the collective. This freedom presupposes a mature mind and the development of certain insights and abilities, whether the individual wants them or not. Freedom also implies a sense of solidarity – which is, in effect, precisely what this book is about: a willingness to miss out on something when it benefits someone else whose need is greater. If no one is willing to give up anything, then life becomes a struggle between individuals to rake in as much as they can for themselves, and that only affords freedom to the very strongest. The dilemma between freedom and coercion is, in a way, at the heart of all pedagogy – we have to be *forced* into education in order to be capable of being *free*. In my opinion, we should remain mindful of this fact in all of our political discussions.

2

Pursuing the Good

In April 1989, my grandmother gave me a poem by Piet Hein as a confirmation present. Hein was a mathematician, designer and inventor, but is best known for his twenty volumes of short poems, many of them in English, called *grooks*. My gran had typed the poem out on green paper, sent it to the poet, and he autographed it and sent it back. At the time, I did not fully understand its meaning, but his words stuck with me and have grown in resonance over the years. I have since learned to appreciate all sorts of modern poetry, and am well aware that many people consider Hein shallow and trivial, but 'my poem' has many fine qualities, despite – or perhaps because of – its straight-forward nature. It is called 'You shouldn't want it all':

> You shouldn't want it all.
> You are only one part.
> You own a world in the world.
> You need to make *it* whole.
> Choose just one path,
> and be as one with it.

Other paths must wait.
We always come back.

Don't hide from troubles.
Confront them here and now.
Finiteness is the very thing
that makes it all worthwhile.
This is the Now you must be,
do and submit to.
That is finiteness.
We never come back.

Several themes in this short poem have influenced me as a psychologist interested in philosophy – especially the idea that it is finiteness 'that makes it all worthwhile'.[1] I also found inspiration in the idea of 'one part', of making your small part of the world whole, something that is only possible if you 'don't want it all'. If you do want it all, life descends into a diffuse and formless mass and is anything but whole. In a similar vein, the theologian and philosopher K.E. Løgstrup, in *The Ethical Demand*, wrote of 'the will to form' which he considered one of the basic phenomena of life, not just for artists, but as 'something basically human, something native to any person even though he may have very little to do with what we usually call art'.[2]

To bestow form on your life is, literally, to practise the existential *art* of living, which is only possible if we are willing to miss out on other things. If your life takes a certain form, it follows logically that it cannot take myriad others – you miss out on them. For Løgstrup, this is not only the case existentially – in the individual's own life – but also applies to how people live their lives with each other. After *The Ethical Demand*, he wrote about the 'tyranny of formlessness' which often reigns when we seek to break free from social rules and conventions. Conventions and polite manners are sometimes considered slightly oppressive – why not just be spontaneous and 'authentic'? Because doing away with conventions does not necessarily lead to freedom (although it can do, as for example with the conventions employed in the past to oppress women). On the contrary, quite often – as the sociologist Richard Sennett noted – it leads to a lack of freedom and further empowers the strong.[3] External forms provide a framework for expressing ourselves freely along with others. In order for something to have lasting importance for the individual on a purely personal level, an existential form of life is necessary.

This, presumably, was also the thinking behind Søren Kierkegaard's famous phrase in *Upbuilding Discourses in Various Spirits* (1847): 'Purity of heart is to will one thing.'[4] He hastens to add that 'If it is to be Possible, That a Man Can Will Only One Thing, Then He Must Will the Good.' On the face of it, this is hard to accept, because it is easy to imagine both malevolent dictators and myopic idealists who 'will one thing', but what they want will not necessarily be good and may inflict harm on others. However, Kierkegaard would assert that 'the Good is one thing', which is why 'The person who wills one thing that is not the Good, he does not truly will one thing. It is a delusion, an illusion, a deception, a self-deception that he wills only one thing. For in his innermost being he is, he is bound to be, double-minded.'[5] Clearly 'one thing' meant something different to Kierkegaard than we would read into the term nowadays. If you monomaniacally seek to achieve something specific – e.g. to exact revenge or to write a bestseller – and you dedicate your whole life to this endeavour, then you are only apparently willing one thing, because your goal is not good *per se*. If it transpired that the person on whom you seek to exact revenge was, in fact, innocent, you would probably start to question the legitimacy of your thirst for vengeance, which would reveal a divided will. It must be something like this that Kierkegaard means – and, as a religious thinker, he would refer to God as the guarantor of good, and thus of the purity of the heart. Strictly speaking, we can only will one thing if it is good we seek, as only the good is complete and indivisible.

If we are to will one thing, we must therefore have the right relationship to the good. If we will good 'for the sake of reward', wrote Kierkegaard, then, basically, we do not will one thing. He shows this with an analogy: 'If a man loves a girl for the sake of her money, who would call him a lover? After all, he does not love the girl but the money.'[6] To will one thing means, then, to will good – not in pursuit of a reward or fear of punishment – but precisely because it is good: 'That the good is its own reward, yes, that is eternally certain. There is nothing so certain, it is not more certain that there is a God, because this is one and the same.'[7] Here, Kierkegaard associates God with the idea that good is a reward in its own right; that good is its own purpose. Whether we agree with this concept of God or not, Kierkegaard shows himself here as a sharp critic of the instrumentalisation so prevalent in our time, when more and more phenomena are deemed to be valuable purely insofar as we stand to gain from them.[8] If we do something to 'get something out of it', then we are strictly speaking not willing one thing, according to Kierkegaard's analysis, and are doomed to remain double-minded. This is because personal motivations and preferences are naturally complex and changeable, whereas only the good is one thing. As a result, 'purity of heart' requires that we learn to will the good for its own sake. According to Kierkegaard, this will not lead to oppression under the yoke of duty, but will set us free: 'So different is it – the person who wills the good in truth, he is the only free person, free through the good. But then someone who wills the good only out of fear of punishment does not will the good in truth, and therefore the good only makes him a slave.'[9]

That purity of heart is to will one thing is not an empirical psychological observation, as I understand it. In reality, our more or less legitimate desires and psychological impulses consist of a range of motives and justifications that we rarely fully comprehend. Rather, it is an existential statement that says something about an ideal set of basic conditions for life, which is why Kierkegaard insists upon the existence of the good. To what extent it is possible to be motivated by the good is another matter, and brings us to psychology. But there is plenty of testimony to the radical importance of the good in life – for example in the book *Dying We Live*, edited by Gollwitzer et al., which collates poignant letters written to their loved ones from people interned by the Nazis and sentenced to death during the Second World War.[10] One young German, potentially with a whole life ahead of him, writes to his parents explaining that he would rather go to his death than join the SS. The punishment for resisting the totalitarian society's demand for enrolment in the Nazi system was execution. Most people would probably acquiesce to save their lives, but here we have someone who could not compromise on his perception of the good, and would rather miss out on the rest of his life than sacrifice his integrity and commitment to ethical ideals. This truly is heroic. Fortunately, we are rarely forced to make such a choice, but it is psychologically interesting – and edifying – that some people manage to maintain purity of the heart in such extreme situations. It is somewhat reminiscent of Luther's famous words of 16 April 1521, when he was accused by the church of having expressed criticism of the papacy and its indulgences: 'Here I stand, I cannot do otherwise.' Both the young German anti-Nazi and Luther seem to be thinking that if they are to continue to be the same person, no matter what form their life takes, then there is no alternative but to stand firm. The question of the nature of this good upon which it is worth standing firm, is, of course, absolutely crucial. As previously mentioned, people may believe that they will one thing, but it is actually something not worth willing – and according to Kierkegaard, they are in fact double-minded. In my own attempt to unravel this in *Standpoints*, I argue that the good is that which has intrinsic value and which we should pursue for its own sake, not in order to achieve something else. In the context of this chapter and this book, the point is that willing something at all, in the existential sense, requires that you learn the art of missing out.

Caring about something

These days, the message most often preached is not Piet Hein's advice about not wanting it all, but the polar opposite. An extreme example is the world-famous American coach Tony Robbins, whose motivational sloganeering I find endlessly fascinating. His definition of success is doing 'what you want to do, when you want, where you want, with whom you want, as much as you want'.[11] This may sound like 'purity of heart', as it points to the significance of willing *something*, but it is in fact the exact opposite – because it is formless, limitless and infinite ('as much as you want'). What if what you want is not good? What if it is not worth wanting? Well, you are still a success as long as you do whatever you want. And what if what you want constantly changes? Well, then you have to keep running from one thing to the other in case you miss out on something better. Kierkegaard's observation that willing one thing *must* be related to good (for only the good is one thing) is highly relevant here. Without an ethical framework, the will is random, controlled solely by the individual's more or less fleeting desires and preferences.

The philosopher Harry Frankfurt, best known for his humorous essay 'On Bullshit', wrote a seminal article in modern philosophy called 'The Importance of What We Care About'.[12] In it, he seeks to elaborate on this existential theme. Rather than focusing on the purely epistemological ('What should I think?') or the purely moral ('How should I act?'), the essay is simply concerned with what we ought to care about in our lives. What has deep, existential meaning?

Frankfurt says that this last question is related to ethics, but not just in a narrow sense, because people care about all sorts of things without necessarily subjecting them to any specifically ethical evaluation. One example of this is provided by a doctor, Lise Gormsen. Upon meeting an old woman with chronic pain in a palliative care ward, Gormsen asked her about her problems and concerns. Surprisingly, the old lady replied that what was worrying her most was not the pains in her body but the fact that she had not pruned her garden roses.[13] Even those without roses in their garden will get the point. Caring for garden roses is not an ethical or moral issue in the traditional sense,[14] but it can nevertheless be meaningful for a person who has devoted time and energy to it. It is this sort of thing, Frankfurt believes, that philosophy needs to be better at acknowledging – i.e. that there are things we care about in life. Furthermore, since we often identify with the things we care about, this accounts for our feeling vulnerable if anything happens to them (for example, if the roses die).

For Frankfurt, it is crucial that caring for something is different from simply having a desire or lust. You may briefly have a craving for something and then forget it a moment later. But you cannot care for something for an isolated moment. It is only possible to care over time, once it becomes part of the way you live your life and your identity – in other words, once you achieve a kind of purity of heart. Frankfurt also stresses that the things we care about are usually outside the influence of our will. We can do our best – we can water, prune and fertilise the roses – but we have no guarantee of success. As a result, caring for something always implies the risk of being disappointed or suffering real grief. This is the price of love, as is often (rightly) said. In turn, there is something liberating about running this risk, in accepting that aspects of the world are beyond our control. As Frankfurt notes, this is a recurring theme in our moral and religious traditions. We are at our best as human beings, he says, when we 'escape ourselves' through reason and love.[15] By deploying reason – which is impersonal in the sense that we all have it – we free ourselves from the prison of subjectivity and egotism. The same applies if we open ourselves up to a love that is personal and relational. The ability to care enables us to surrender to something else (for example, the better argument or the loved one), and in doing so to endow our life with form and our deeds with integrity. However, it also involves a risk of disappointment and defeat – perhaps it will turn out that my argument is weaker than that of the person I am debating; or perhaps the person I love will leave me. In these circumstances, we should, again, practise willing one thing – the good – by placing greater emphasis on truth than on winning the debate or on the fact that our love may remain unrequited. Purity of heart is to will one thing. Not to gain something in return – in which case, it is not purity of heart, but a financial transaction – but because what we care about is worth wanting *per se* and therefore is in itself one thing.

The myth of human potential

Once Kierkegaard had identified the existential significance of willing one thing, it became clear that to do so is associated with major risks. It might even be said that it is almost certainly doomed to fail. Not because the good is not one thing – according to Kierkegaard, it is so by definition – but because human beings are fallible and rarely achieve completely pure hearts, except in rare cases like that of the young German mentioned above. The risk is therefore that in willing one thing we end up disappointed, because we fail somewhere along the way. But it is a risk worth taking. It is the risk we run when we get married and say yes to a lifelong commitment, despite knowing full well that almost half of all marriages end up in divorce. It is the risk inherent in willing one thing in a loving relationship to another person, and perhaps living with them for years, only for our spouse to be unfaithful and perhaps even leave one day. Were all those years wasted? Were we taken for a ride? Kierkegaard would console us by saying no. If we will the good in a relationship, then it has a validity that does not just disappear along with the other party, even if we feel let down. By daring to miss out on all the other tantalising opportunities for love that might present themselves along the way, we make ourselves vulnerable. But the alternatives are worse. One alternative is to try to avoid caring for anything in particular because we do not wish to place any restraints on ourselves and would prefer to experience as much as possible. In the Kierkegaardian sense, this leads to a kind of aesthetic despair, and life becomes one long hunt for the next experiential fix. We live a life with no particular form because we try to will not one thing, but everything – an endeavour doomed to failure. The other alternative is to seek to extinguish the will completely, i.e. to want as little as possible because the risk of disappointment involved in wanting something specific is too high. Not daring to want anything is probably the lowest point a person can reach – the restless experience-hunter at least has his or her pleasures and diversions. One of the key characteristics of depression is what doctors and psychologists call *anhedonia*, the symptoms of which include a lack of desire. A small number of ascetics may be able to eliminate desire without too many ill effects, but for the rest of us, a lack of desire (which is after all, psychologically motivating) would be extremely debilitating. For most people, such a lack would be worse than the disappointment of not achieving what you are striving for. But that just makes striving for what is right all the more important.

A central theme of our modern concept of humanity is *the inner*: that what we strive for should come from within; that it is a matter of realising ourselves and our full potential. Nowadays, according to the psychoanalyst Adam Phillips – who has written one of the few books on the importance of missing out – we are haunted by the myth of our own potential.[16] As Plato reported in the *Apology*, upon being sentenced to death Socrates said: 'You would have even less faith in me if I said that there is, in fact, no greater good for a human being than to spend every day discussing what it means to be a decent person and all the other issues you have heard me hold forth on in my studies of my own and others' lives: our life is only worth living when we are able to subject it to critical examination.' In other words, Socrates believed that life is not worth living unless it is subjected to scrutiny. By the 'examined life' he was not referring to the kind of modern navel-gazing people indulge in when they look inward and seek to understand their unique life and opportunities. Rather, Socrates wished to discuss what constitutes 'a decent person' and how to become one. In ancient Greece, philosophy was not a vehicle for 'personal development', a tool to realise our truest self. Rather, it was about justice, beauty and goodness – about being the best

possible human being. In his book, Adam Phillips refor-
mulates Socrates' insight to argue that the non-lived life
is worth examining. What does he mean?

Phillips' premise is that the non-lived life – the life that
we live in our imaginations, in art and in our dreams – is
often more important to us than the one we actually
live. This is not to defend irresponsible escapism – on
the contrary, it is a recognition that, to a large extent,
it is the things that we opt out of and omit that make
us who we are. Existentialists claim that individuals are
defined by their actions. They are not completely wrong,
but we must also take into account that we are defined
just as much by what we *do not* do. We are formed by
what we miss out on, not just by the things we do. Only
in this way does life achieve the form that Løgstrup
considered to be existentially crucial. However, as
Phillips has learned from his patients, missing out has
become difficult: 'Once the promise of immortality, of
being chosen, was displaced by the promise of more
life – the promise, as we say, of getting more out of life
– the unlived life became a haunting presence in a life
legitimated by nothing more than the desire to live it.'[17]
If *this* life is the only one we can hope to live, then we
become almost obsessed with living and experiencing
as much as possible. In turn, we also become obsessed
with not missing out on anything, which is not only dis-
tressing for the individual, but ultimately destructive to
society and culture – because how can we possibly satisfy an endless craving for more and more? How do we
apply the brakes and say that enough is enough? Phillips
cites the sociologist and cultural critic Philip Rieff, who
wrote that the path to morality and culture's deepest
secret is via knowledge of what to avoid. But nowadays

it is deemed better not to avoid anything at all! I recently heard an interesting radio programme in which young cyber-geeks discussed the digitalisation of sexual life via the internet. New opportunities for sexual pleasure, e.g. robots and previously unimaginable forms of pornography, are popping up all the time. All of the participants thought it was important to try as many of them as possible. And why not? It is well-nigh impossible to reject something new and exciting without sounding dull and reactionary. I have myself been interested in the appeal of the 'new' ever since I read an interview with the techno group The Overlords while I was still at school. They said that if they had to choose between something old that was good and something new that was worse, they would choose the latter, simply because it was new. I wouldn't contend that this position – which, strictly speaking, is absurd – is universally accepted, but I would maintain that our fear of missing out (FOMO) means that many of us veer closer to it than we might care to admit.

You can't always get what you want

But why should we want to experience as many things as possible? What do we stand to gain from all of these new experiences? There is no prize for the person who comes first or does the most – indeed, we all cross the finishing line at the same point, because death awaits us all. The analyses in this book so far indicate that the urge to try it all stems from the idea of an infinite, insatiable *more*, which is an intrinsic part of modern capitalist culture. This idea takes on an almost religious force when coupled to the 'Just do it!' philosophy and the imperative to do as much as possible before you die. However, if the historical reading of the emergence of this idea is valid, it is not an intrinsic part of human nature. On the contrary, many cultures – perhaps most – have historically been based not on doing more, but on playing a productive part in natural cycles. The first significant historical transition came with the emergence of agriculture, when humans started to refine and optimise their relationship with nature. The second came with the Industrial Revolution and the idea of accumulation, as analysed by the sociologist Max Weber in his book on the Protestant ethic.[18] According to Weber, the highest good in the Protestant work ethic is to acquire more and more money – a purely instrumental phenomenon that becomes a goal in itself at the expense of individual happiness. With the advent of the later *new* capitalism in the twentieth century, industrial society's ethics based on duty or needs gradually merged with consumer society's pleasure-based ethics. Now, it is not only the *accumulation* of capital that is a goal in itself, but also the *realisation* of capital, via consumption and self-realisation. Everyone now has the right to whatever they want, whenever they want (albeit within the law).

In 1969, in the wake of that era's counter-cultural rebellion (which, in reality, involved only a tiny minority of the population), Mick Jagger of the Rolling Stones sang: 'You can't always get what you want / But if you try sometimes well you just might find / you get what you need.' This chapter has sought to provide an existential reason why, when told that you cannot always get what you want, you should respond 'And a good thing, too!' Human desires are diverse and changeable, especially in a media and consumer society where we are constantly assailed by temptations and calls to action, and where the mere fact of having a desire makes it legitimate. All of this makes it difficult to distinguish significant desires from insignificant ones. It is hard to make a case for settling for less and difficult to really care about something in a binding, lasting way. Kierkegaard's talk of purity of heart may sound pompous and alien to modern ears, as we are accustomed to looking inside ourselves to find direction in life and the meaning of things, but perhaps his words can help modern readers to realise that there is a world beyond ourselves, in which something can be good or bad, independently of our wishes and preferences. And perhaps it could be liberating to pursue the good, regardless of potential personal gain. If there is any value in this idea, then the ambition of realising as many of our own desires as possible is far from liberating. On the contrary, in doing so we run the risk of becoming slaves to our desires. To be liberated, we must be prepared to miss out – in other words, we must will one thing rather than will everything and succumb to an amorphous formlessness.

3

The Value of Moderation

Philosophers and theologians have spent millennia pondering humankind's capacity as an ethical and moral species.[1] In recent times, they have been joined by anthropologists, sociologists, psychologists, economists and researchers from other disciplines who have also conducted studies of that which – probably more than anything else – distinguishes us as a species: our capacity to act morally (and therefore immorally). The economists' perspectives have been particularly noteworthy because they have long wielded a great deal of social influence in terms of defining our understanding of humankind. Their standard model – sometimes called *homo economicus* – is based on us all being rational individuals who, in any given situation, will act out of self-interest in order to maximise personal gain. In other words, this perspective sees us all as cost-benefit analysers, out to rake in as much as possible of what we want, with as little effort as possible. It leaves little room for the notion of humans as ethical beings, at least not if ethics is understood to involve self-sacrifice and unconditional generosity; that is, if acting ethically sometimes involves giving something without necessarily expecting anything in return.

In recent decades, this economic perspective has been challenged – not only by other economists, but also by psychologists, who have conducted multiple experiments showing that, in practice, we often act quite differently than would be expected if we all really were just *homo economicus*. The psychologist Daniel Kahneman even received a Nobel Prize in economics in 2002 for his work in this area (there is no Nobel Prize for psychology).[2] One of the most famous experiments challenging this concept of human nature is the ultimatum game. It has many variations, but the basic idea involves two subjects, one of whom is handed a sum of money, say £100, and has to decide how it should be shared. She is free to choose to keep it all for herself, share it equally with the other subject, or divide it up between them differently. The other participant then decides whether to accept or reject the sum offered. If he accepts, then the money is split in the way the proposer suggested. If he rejects the proposal, neither receives any money. According to the standard economics model of human behaviour, the experiment says that it is rational for the receiver to accept any amount offered. If he is offered only a penny, and the proposer keeps £99.99, it is still better to walk away with a penny than with nothing. Even if he is offered nothing (i.e. the proposer intends to keep all of the money), there is no rational reason to reject this decision, because the proposer missing out on the money makes no difference to what the recipient would have received. But reality does not work like that. Experiments have shown that we have a strong proclivity to reject anything that we perceive as unfair –

even when we lose out personally by doing so. At least, this is the case in some cultural contexts, although there are significant variations around the world. In Northern Europe, many people will refuse to accept an amount they consider unfair (because they think that the other person is receiving disproportionately more), even if it means missing out completely. In some cases, it seems that fairness – and perhaps the desire to punish a miserly adversary – is a stronger motivation than the desire to 'get the most out of it'.

The most interesting aspect of the ultimatum game is whether the person who is offered the sum of money, or none at all, rejects or accepts it. An even simpler version, which only looks at the person making the offer, is called the dictator game. In this version, the proposer is completely sovereign and has dictatorial power to share the sum, while the other party has no influence and is forced to take whatever is offered. If he is offered nothing, well, that is just the way it is; and if he is offered half, then that is fine too, most people seem to think. Again, the standard economic model would predict that the proposer (the dictator) would want to keep as much as possible. If she has £100 to allocate, she should keep all of it and offer the other player nothing. In practice, however, the results are often different, and may restore a little of our childhood faith in humanity. The fact is that many players choose to give the other a slice of the pie – sometimes even a fairly large one. Christoph Engel, director of the Max Planck Institute for Research on Collective Goods, based in Bonn, has summarised the results of over 100 published studies of the dictator game. He calculates that, on average, 'the dictator' chooses to give the other player approximately

28 per cent of the sum total[3] – and bear in mind that this is to a complete stranger, somebody they will probably never meet again and to whom they owe nothing. Only just over one third of 'dictators' keep all the money to themselves, while around 16 per cent share the amount equally. And it is worth noting that 5 per cent give it all away.

Results like these have, of course, been the subject of intense discussion. Although there is no consensus on how to interpret them, it does seem that people are often much more generous – even to strangers – than the standard economic model would have us believe. Using the terminology employed in this book, it would appear that many of us are willing to miss out on something we would otherwise have had, even when we hold out no expectation of a reward at some point in the future. One interpretation of this is that we are fundamentally ethical beings who do not always think about what is best for ourselves in each and every situation, but have a sense of justice that means we are prepared to take other people into consideration, including strangers, and to share with them. In other words, we are able to establish an overview of a situation and assess what is fair, relatively independently of our own potential benefit. This should, in a way, be taken for granted, but these results have become famous, and led to Nobel Prizes, for a reason. As mentioned earlier, the economic understanding that forms the scientific backbone of modern society is based on an entirely different view of humankind – one that says that we are all creatures who want *more, more, more*, and will only do things that benefit us. This makes these results encouraging to those of us who still consider moderation and generosity to be ethical virtues. It is precisely the ethical value inherent in moderation and missing out that is the focus of this chapter.

The lily and the bird

One of the lessons of these economic experiments is that the idea of individuals as egocentric atoms, within a society motivated solely by self-interest, is both simplistic and misguided. Of course, we do act in an egotistical and selfish manner in various situations, but we are not hardwired to do so. It is not 'our nature'. People want to be generous, cooperative and helpful to others if they live in an environment that facilitates it. Many psychologists now claim that not only are we in fact relational creatures who seek out company, but we are probably like that from the very outset. The famous developmental psychologist Donald Winnicott radically asserted that, strictly speaking, there is no such thing as an infant,[4] because the infant is nothing without its caregivers. The smallest developmental psychology unit is not the child – which Winnicott considered almost an abstraction – but the child-and-caregiver (in his time, he referred exclusively to the mother as caregiver, but nowadays we recognise that men are capable of playing this role). The child is basically relational, interacts with the world, and engages in inter-subjective relations. Only later, and quite gradually, does the child build up an understanding of themselves as a separate subject and begin to hide their feelings – and, later still, even pretend that they have certain feelings without actually having them. Development psychologists after Winnicott have mapped out the fascinating interactions in which young children participate from their earliest moments, illustrating that people basically 'face outward' in their relations with the world and with other people. Western philosophy's idea that each of us is an inner, closed, psychological space is quite remarkably different from most other cultures' views of human nature. Nevertheless, it is thinking like this that has formed the basis for the economic view of humankind, because if each of us is a small, enclosed world of our own, then we are logically self-sufficient and should optimise whatever wishes and preferences we have at any price. In my book *Standpoints* I called this a kind of 'passive nihilism': the idea that the world is devoid of meaning and value makes these concepts things that you have to create subjectively in your 'inner world'.[5] However, if instead we see ourselves as relational, then we know that we are actually nothing without others – and not just abstract others, but specific individuals with whom we have relationships and share a common history.

This whole network of human relations, which constitutes the fundamental material of our lives, Løgstrup called interdependence – a basic condition of mutual dependence in which we owe each other our very existence. For this network of relationships to function, we must learn the art of self-restraint right from the start. We cannot demand to have our own way all the time, just because we think our ideas are brilliant. We have to acquire a certain reserve, learn to listen to others and sometimes even hold ourselves back. Laid out in black and white like this, this notion sounds well-nigh archaic, because it is almost the opposite of what we are encouraged to do today. We are all supposed to

The Joy of Missing Out

be proactive, assertive and constantly self-developing, reading self-help books and taking self-development courses. One formula for success, as mentioned in the previous chapter, is to do 'what you want to do, when you want, where you want, with whom you want, as much as you want' – at least according to one American 'life coach'. It sounds even more archaic if, as in the previous chapter, we revert to Kierkegaard and his 'formula for success' (not that he would ever have called it that), as expressed in his various texts and speeches about the lily and the bird.[6] In these pieces, Kierkegaard examines what people can learn from lilies and birds. His answer may seem weighty and old-fashioned, but it also has its own peculiar poetry: 'silence, obedience, joy!' With the lily and the bird as teachers, Kierkegaard implores humankind to, above all, learn silence, to learn to refrain from speaking. We must learn this because humans possess the power of speech – otherwise, there would be no reason to learn the art of silence. Since the lily and the bird do not possess the power of speech, their silence is not an art, but humankind must learn it. Why, you might ask? So that we can learn to listen!

Kierkegaard was not saying that people should be exactly like the lily, the bird or any other organism that lacks the power of speech, but he did think that they served as good examples from an ethical point of view. Of course, people are far more complex creatures than lilies or birds, and this is also why we are capable of experiencing deeper suffering than them. Our suffering does not stem from our ability to talk – 'for that is a virtue', he writes – 'but from our inability to keep silent'.[7]

As a Christian thinker, Kierkegaard believed that

The Value of Moderation

silence expresses reverence for God. Although this is the interpretation of a man of faith, I think Kierkegaard's analysis includes a more generally applicable insight: namely, that there is a reality and that it consists of other people, but also of a greater natural order to which we should listen, instead of always talking and filling time and space with our subjective desires and observations. The Norwegian writer Karl Ove Knausgård addresses this in his long essay *Om foråret* (Spring). In one passage, he describes his daughter, who is at a party with her classmates, eating sausages, which leads him to the following poetic reflection:

> I remained where I was, standing with one hand in my pocket and the other around the handle of the pram. The triviality of the ketchup and mustard bottles, the blackened hot dogs, the camping table where the soft drinks were lined up, was almost inconceivable there beneath the stars, in the dancing light of the bonfire. It was as if I was standing in a banal world and gazing into a magical one, as if our lives played out in the borderland between two parallel realities.
>
> We come from far away, from terrifying beauty, for a newborn child who opens its eyes for the first time, is like a star, is like a sun, but we live our lives amid pettiness and stupidity, in the world of burned hot dogs and wobbly camping tables. The great and terrifying beauty does not abandon us, it is there all the time, in everything that is always the same, in the sun and the stars, in the bonfire and the darkness, in the blue carpet of flowers beneath the tree. It is of no use to us, it is too big for us, but we can look at it, and we can bow before it.[8]

Yes, it is sentimental. But how else would we express the fact that there is a world, a nature, a wholeness, that we did not create, which 'is of no use to us', and which we can only look at in silence and prostrate ourselves in front of? I see Knausgård as a contemporary voice trying to express the same thing Kierkegaard wanted to say, in a more archaic manner, with the story of the lily and the bird. Both are talking about something that we have almost lost the vocabulary to discuss – a kind of awe at the fact that the world exists, an awe that also has an ethical dimension.

This also applies to the kind of obedience Kierkegaard identifies, by which, of course, he means obedience to God, but which can also be interpreted more generally as a way of living that accentuates the factual, accepting that there is something that cannot be changed, and which we therefore must 'obey', even though we might prefer 'alternative facts' that support our own case.

Finally, there is the joy of being, which Kierkegaard writes about in a manner almost reminiscent of the 'gratitude exercises' in contemporary positive psychology: 'that thou didst become a man; that thou canst see – only think, that thou canst see! – that thou canst hear, thou canst smell, thou canst taste, thou canst feel; that the sun shines upon thee . . . and for thy sake, that when the sun is weary the moon then begins, then the stars are lit'. He continues to enumerate many phenomena over which we should rejoice, before finally concluding: 'If this is nothing to be glad of, then there is nothing to be glad of.'[9]

According to Kierkegaard (and Knausgård, in his way), silence, obedience and joy are demands placed on humankind that endow us with ethical character and dignity, but are also predicated on self-restraint rather than overstepping boundaries. It is not just the

The Value of Moderation

Christian thinker Kierkegaard who writes about this. The Danish cultural commentator and radical socialist Otto Gelsted wrote beautifully about it too, in his poem 'Salmer' (Psalms), published in the collection *Enetaler* (Monologues) from 1922. This time it is not the lily or the bird but the trees that serve as an ethical and existential inspiration:

Gazing at your navel
is but a poor life,
picking our sores
a bad pastime.
Look at the trees in the fence,
they are well worth seeing.
How tall, proud and silent
they all act.

Like animals who huddle together
against the wet of the night,
the trees sway
in the sun's evening sheen,
so credible and safe
in their costume of leaves
like animals with shaggy backs.
Dust, yes, they are of dust!

Some people say that the truth is poetic (while others might add that it is too bad, therefore, that people cannot stand poetry!). In any case, some truths appear to be better suited to transmission by aesthetic means (e.g. poetry) than via linear or scientific prose. This is perhaps especially true of the ethical/existential identification of the value of a modest life, in what Kierkegaard called silence, obedience and joy.

The moderate character in politics and ethics

Further back in time, Aristotle, too, was deeply interested in the ethical value of moderation. His ethics of
virtue played a major role in *Standpoints*, so I will make
do with a quick introduction to his thinking here.[10]
The basic idea of the ethics of virtue is that humans are
creatures who, like everything else in the universe, must
be understood on the basis of their purpose. Humans
are the only creatures endowed with both theoretical
and practical reasoning, and as such they have the ability to reflect scientifically and philosophically about the
world, but also the ability to act in a morally responsible
manner. According to Aristotle, there is intrinsic value
in having and using these abilities. The character traits
necessary to make the most of human nature and thrive
in life (which the Greeks called *eudaimonia*) are known
as the virtues. A virtue, then, is something that enables
the realisation of an inner purpose, whether it is a knife
(where the virtue is to cut well, which is quite clearly the
defining property of a good knife) or a person (in whom
the virtues may be much more diverse and difficult to
define). To understand a person, we must therefore
understand the virtues that enable him or her to be good
(just as a knife can only be understood if we know what
a knife is intended to do – namely, cut well).

In Aristotle, the virtues are ideally positioned between
two polar opposites, often expressed using the phrase
'the virtue is the mean between two vices'. For example,
courage is an ethical virtue – something that, according to
Aristotle, is necessary in order to live a full, flourishing life
– poised somewhere between cowardice on the one hand

The Value of Moderation

and arrogance on the other. Being brave is not the same
as being reckless or entirely free from anxiety and wor-
ries, rather it is a question of daring to do the right thing,
even if you fear doing so. Cowards lack the courage to do
anything, while the arrogant throw themselves headlong
into all sorts of rash actions. According to the ethics of
virtue, both are flawed. A similar analysis can be applied
to the other virtues, which implies that moderation –
defined as the ability to strike a sensible balance between
extremes – is in itself a key virtue. The good person
knows, for example, that generosity is good – certainly
better than stinginess. However, giving everything away
is perhaps not quite so wise if it renders you unable to
feed yourself and your children. The moderate strikes
a balance between stinginess and boundless generosity,
between cowardice and rashness, and so forth. The Greek
word for moderation is *sophrosyne*, which can also be
translated in a multitude of other ways (as self-control, a
measured approach, etc.), and it played a key role for the
ancient thinkers. In one fragment, Heraclitus (who lived
long before Aristotle) even claimed that *sophrosyne* is the
most important virtue of all, which makes sense in light
of the idea of the 'virtue in the middle'.

In recent times, however, there have been few philosophical or scientific studies of the ethical value of
moderation. One exception is the philosopher Harry
Clor's book *On Moderation*, which explicitly sets
out to defend this unfashionable, ancient virtue in a
modern world.[11] Clor is interested in moderation both
as it relates to a moderate political practice that seeks
to improve society gradually, without risky utopian
ventures or revolutions, but also as an ethical virtue or
a form of ethical character. In terms of politics, Clor

53

stresses that being moderate is not simply about balancing between two extremes in the simple arithmetical sense. A moderate politician (which he sees as an ideal) 'builds consensus and unifies; he or she seeks agreements across partisan lines and speaks to the people in a nonconfrontational, noninflammatory way intended to be unifying'.[12]

Clor compares political moderation with thoughtful scientific research, a field of human activity in which it is important to assume a non-partisan approach to complex questions and to spend time understanding various conflicting perspectives. To make a sensible judgement – be it in politics, ethics, law or science – we must suspend the urge to enforce a certain attitude and learn to listen to other parties (the Kierkegaardian silence) in order to arrive at a reasonable conclusion. However, this is rarely the ideal that we see practised in modern political contexts. Instead, political discourse is dominated by the quick, clever remark – sometimes on Twitter – designed to signal dynamism and strength. Most people do not cultivate the ability to question their own views when engaged in political discussion. However, if politics is about balancing many different considerations and benefits, as Clor argues, then this is indeed a skill we should promote. Political moderation is about respect for pluralism and the ability to make balanced decisions that take into consideration a wide range of concerns. Clor thinks that a classical humanities education in particular can help us to understand the world from many different perspectives. This is a view shared by a number of philosophers (in particular, Martha Nussbaum) who in recent years have emphasised the importance of literature and other art forms in this context.

The Value of Moderation

If we leave aside political moderation and turn to moderation as a character trait in itself, we see that it is also crucial for ethics. Clor goes so far as to claim that moderation and character may be considered synonymous, in that to be of good character implies the ability to say no to your own impulses and resist temptation. He believes that, ultimately, we *are* our character. This corresponds to Phillips' psychological analysis discussed in the previous chapter – that we are defined at least as much by what we *do not* do as by what we do. Character is about, among other things, the ability to resist, to opt out, to say no. While the concept of character is complex, it contains within it at least two aspects that are ethically relevant. One is discussed by Clor and others (going back to Aristotle), and relates to the ability to control impulses. Without this ability, we lack integrity and cannot be reliable moral agents. If we always act on every sudden impulse, then in a sense we do not act at all, since we are passively driven and determined. We only have free will to the extent that we are able to distance ourselves from our impulses, assess them in the light of our values and other considerations, and then make a decision. The second aspect of character is not so much about making decisions in individual, specific situations where we ought to be able to say no and exercise self-control, but more about the overall shape that a life can take. The French philosopher Paul Ricoeur described this as a kind of self-constancy (in his major work *Oneself as Another*).[13] The concept of self-constancy played a role in my book *Stand Firm*, which levelled criticism at the many cultural practices that impel us toward self-development, flexibility and change for the sake of change, and which therefore threaten our self-constancy – in other words, that aspect of us that remains the same and transcends time and context. If you do not strive for self-constancy, others cannot count on you. What is your incentive to keep your promises, for example, if you are no longer the same person you were when you made them?

According to Ricoeur, to achieve self-constancy we must reflect on our life as a whole, and the best way to do this is to look at it as a narrative. In a sense, our lives consist of *stories* that we must interpret and tell in order to endow our existence with form. Many of us keep a journal or diary or fill photo albums, and so on, in order to put together the pieces of the jigsaw puzzle of life. In contemporary psychology, we refer to this as *narrative identity*, but this is often just a modern way of expressing the older concept of character.[14] Ricoeur's point, then, is that people are only moral, in the strict sense, when they relate to their lives as a whole or as a unit that extends backward in time and is best understood as a coherent narrative. Even though this is a different (*diachronic*) aspect of character than the aforementioned (*synchronic*) aspect, both are predicated on our willingness to miss out. This is because, if we insist on trying out every possible identity and narrative throughout our lives, self-constancy becomes impossible. In a culture fascinated by youth, which also lavishes endless resources on perpetual self-development, striving after eternal youth and never-ending experiments with identity may sound attractive. The developmental psychologist Erik Erikson believed that youth ends with a moratorium, after which your identity is determined by certain obligations. Today, however, this moratorium can last almost our entire lives – indeed, some psychologists encourage us to live in a never-ending identity laboratory. One such is the postmodern psychologist Kenneth Gergen, who in a famous book on reality and relationships suggests that we should explore many different narratives about our lives rather than commit to any particular truth about who we are.[15] This is the exact opposite of both self-constancy and character. It is to live the life of a chameleon. You may change colour because fashion dictates it, because another hue is just more opportune, or perhaps simply because you are bored. Can this form the basis for an ethical life? Not if the proponents of moderation introduced in this chapter are right.

In his book *On Settling*, cited in the previous chapter, Robert Goodin refers to a scene from the film *Goodfellas*, where a mother says to her son, 'Why don't you find a nice girl?', to which the son replies, 'I do. Almost every night.' Following up, the mother says insistently, 'But I mean one you can settle down with.' And the son responds, 'I do. Almost every night.'[16] It's a humorous exchange, but illustrates the lack of ethical obligation in constantly wanting something more, something different and something new – in this case, in the context of love and sex. If this becomes a consistent attitude to life, we quickly descend into a kind of Kierkegaardian aesthetic despair, destined to remain forever dissatisfied because we feel that something better awaits us around the next corner. This not only leads us into a state of despair (see the existential discussion in the previous chapter); it also makes it difficult for us to live an ethical life based on obligations, which necessarily involves a certain degree of loyalty, trust, self-sacrifice and other similar virtues. All of these values are linked to moderation and a willingness to miss out on what may appear superficially exciting.

Everything in moderation

Oscar Wilde famously proclaimed that he could resist everything – except temptation! We might add in a similar vein that you should do everything in moderation – including moderation! I say this in order to emphasise that the purpose of moderation, in an ethical sense, is not some form of asceticism or self-torment. The goal is, of course, to live well and properly as human beings, and moderation is just one among many components of an ethical life. It is a central component – possibly even a cardinal virtue – but moderation can, like anything else, be overdone to an unhealthy degree. It can become sacrosanct, puritanical and unbearable, not only for the moderates themselves, but for those around them. So we must remember always to be moderate in our moderation!

How do we determine the right kind of moderation in a particular situation? If we were to consult Aristotle – my usual starting point when exploring issues involving ethics and the individual – he would say that only a well-cultivated emotional life can help us with this, in other words one in which emotions do not stand in opposition to reason, but provide reliable knowledge about the world around us. Fear can, of course, inform us of the presence of something dangerous and terrible (but it can also be pathological, i.e. when we fear something innocent and harmless). A person's guilt can inform us that they are indeed guilty because they have violated a moral code (but blame can also be unfounded and tortuous). And a person's pride – to use a more positive feeling – can tell us that they have done something significant and admirable, of which they have reason to be proud (again, this feeling may not be justified, as it is certainly possible for people to feel proud of something when they absolutely should not). The point is that our emotions are cognitive – or at least, they have the potential to be so. But like all other sources of knowledge, our emotional life can also lead us astray. As such, the emotional socialisation that occurs throughout life, but especially in childhood, is incredibly important. When learning the art of self-restraint, it is not sufficient to know intellectually that we should share with others, let them have their say, commit ourselves to a particular form of life and miss out on others, etc. We also have to be able to *feel* it – not necessarily because the emotions possess any authority *per se*, but because an ethics that does not leave an imprint on the body, one that is not felt, will not have great potential for translation into action. Ultimately, ethics is not an abstract, intellectual game, but a practical venture. It is about acting – and refraining from acting. Having a moderate moral character that enables ethical action requires a well-cultivated emotional life, in which we have learned to rejoice in the good, fear the awful and feel guilt when we have done wrong. In this way, moral feelings help to frame and define the situations in which we find ourselves, so that we are better able to understand them and act appropriately. An immoderate over-sensitivity, on the other hand, will cloud our awareness of moral reality. With this in mind, let's now grapple with the psychological dimensions of missing out.

4

Marshmallows and Treadmills

One of the best-known outcomes of a psychology experiment occurred by chance. Originally, the lead researcher, Walter Mischel, wanted to know how preschool children would react in a situation where they had to choose either an immediate reward (a biscuit, pretzel or marshmallow) or a larger reward later (e.g. two biscuits), on the condition that they wait up to twenty minutes before eating the first one. The children were allowed to choose their reward, and then had to sit alone in a room at Bing Nursery School at Stanford University. The experiment was conducted in the 1960s. In his book about it many years later, Mischel describes vividly how the children struggled not to eat the first reward.[1] They displayed great ingenuity in their attempts to divert their own attention from the tempting treats. In a certain sense, the tempted individual struggling with their own desires is fundamental to our self-understanding, and goes all the way back to Adam and Eve in the Garden of Eden. The experiment illustrates the unique complexity of human psychology. We may want to eat something delicious right away, but at the same time we may have a conflicting desire to not eat it – perhaps because we are on a diet, or because we would prefer to eat more later on. The latter was the option presented to the children to put their will-power to the test.

The children's creative avoidance strategies are fascinating enough in their own right, but the experiment became world famous because the researchers went back to the same children several years later and asked their parents about their children's subsequent behaviour and personality traits. The findings were striking, and the experiment has been known ever since as *the marshmallow test* (despite several other treats being on offer). More than 550 took the test in the period 1968–74, and the experiment has been repeated many times since. The fascinating finding is that a significant positive correlation emerged between the amount of time the children were able to wait during the experiment and their results in SAT tests (the entrance qualification for American higher education) later in life. Not only that, but the ability to delay gratification was shown to be fairly closely related to a number of other characteristics when the subjects reached adulthood (27–32), for example in terms of self-esteem, stress management and the general ability to achieve important goals. It even turned out that the children who were classed as 'high delayers' had significantly lower than average BMIs as adults, and so were less prone to obesity.

It sounds incredible that the ability of relatively small children to delay gratification in a simple laboratory experiment should reveal so much about their long-term development. It was, of course, this surprising discovery that made the marshmallow test world famous. The test has since passed into popular culture and been reproduced many times on various television programmes. Inevitably, it has formed the basis of self-help books, including *Do Not Eat the Marshmallow ... Yet! The Secret to Sweet Success in Work and Life*.[2] I began this book by describing our culture as an ecological niche in which we are constantly invited to do and to consume. We inhabit a cultural landscape full of temptations – no wonder many of us want to learn about self-control and its importance. However, before readers submit themselves and their offspring to marshmallow tests, it is worth remembering that Mischel's research was all about statistical correlations. In principle, the results say nothing about individuals. Even a child who does poorly in the test and shovels the treat down without delay, may well turn out to be a healthy, slim and clever adult, perfectly capable of complying with the norms of the competition society – if indeed such norms are worth complying with (I must admit that I have a soft spot for the kids who do not wait). Statistical averages say nothing about individuals, and published statistical data often has the side-effect of scaring people unnecessarily, depending on how the figures are presented. For example, it is a fact that smokers are twenty-four times more likely to develop lung cancer than non-smokers. This represents an enormous increase in the risk of serious illness, but it is also a fact that, among smokers, 'only' about 16 per cent of men and 9 per cent of women develop lung cancer.[3] Smoking is the cause of approximately 90 per cent of cases of lung cancer, but the vast majority of smokers do not develop the disease – fortunately. I am not trying to downplay the risks of smoking, but to demonstrate that statistics can be displayed in many ways, depending on what you want to show. Whether an individual who smokes will actually end up with lung cancer is not something that we can extrapolate from the knowledge that there is a relative increase in the risk for the population as a whole. The same applies to children taking the marshmallow test. However, in our modern optimisation culture, universal statistical findings are transformed in the blink of an eye into educational concepts and self-help books to boost the individual's self-control – regardless of circumstances.

A recent repeat of the marshmallow test calls it into question for different reasons. The psychologist Celeste Kidd and her colleagues invited a group of children to take the test more than thirty years after the Mischel experiment. This time, however, half the children were first exposed to an unpredictable researcher who did not keep her promises, the other half to a reliable one.[4] The results very clearly showed that approximately two-thirds of those who were welcomed by a reliable adult were able to wait the full fifteen minutes for the double reward, compared to only one (out of fourteen) in the other group. The researchers concluded that it is not only self-control – in abstract terms – that is essential to human life, but also our trust in the world and other people. In other words, it is apparently very much a matter of context (is the world trustworthy?), rather than a single characteristic (self-control) that we can isolate in the individual. The new study in no way detracts from Mischel's original work, but it adds a new layer to its interpretation, one that invites us to think about people's success in ways that are other than purely individualistic. It implies that we must also look at the conditions and environments around them, not just at their 'inner' psychological characteristics.[5] Anybody who grows up in an unpredictable world of chaos and broken promises quickly learns not to rely on anything, and will see no reason to hesitate when confronted with the treat – just think of the old adage that a bird in the hand is worth two in the bush. What may at first look like poor self-control can, in some cases, reflect experience and rationality.

The opportunist

I started this chapter on the psychological dimension by recalling the marshmallow test because it tells us something about the importance of missing out here and now to obtain more later. It takes self-control to miss out – and, according to Mischel, self-control can be trained like a muscle. The ability to exercise self-control allegedly has greater significance for the individual's future success than, for example, a high IQ (again, statistically speaking). I definitely think that there is something in this, but beyond querying the individualistic interpretation of the marshmallow test – which plays down the importance of an environment that inspires trust – I also believe that it is worth casting a critical eye over the basic premise of the experiment. Why should we develop self-control and miss out on a small reward here and now? In the test, the motivation is to receive a *bigger* reward later on. Based on the logic of the experiment, human beings are creatures motivated by reward (and punishment). But what about situations in which we have to keep ourselves in check and delay gratification *with-*

out any expectation of a greater reward later on? For example, imagine a child (or an adult, for that matter) on a picnic with a friend who has lost her picnic basket. The child has four marshmallows left and would like to tuck into them all, but is considering whether it would perhaps be better to give half of the marshmallows – or at least one – to her friend. Most parents would probably hope that in a situation like this, their child would share. I know that I am proud when my own children spontaneously act like this – and when they do not, I strongly urge them to do so. Share and share alike! It may well be that it does actually pay to share – the friend may reciprocate at some point – but it may not. Either way, standard moral socialisation teaches us that the very question 'will it pay?' has no bearing on the moral qualities of an action.[6] Only selfish opportunists ask themselves this question all the time. The opportunist may well be the ideal in the so-called competition state, but opportunism is basically the polar opposite of true moral fortitude. The job of the modern competition state has become to encourage us to consider ourselves (jointly) responsible for our own competencies and self-development, both in the education system and at work. From this springs the ideal of the opportunist, who seizes chances, assumes responsibility for their own learning and pushes their own agenda in competition with everybody else.[7]

The thinking that underpins the marshmallow test might be said to imply the same opportunistic and instrumental logic. It is all about learning to wait for the sake of a greater reward later on. This is a purely quantitative perspective, and by adopting it we run the risk of neglecting the qualitative dimension, in which some actions are simply more correct than others. This brings us back to Kierkegaard's existential axiom that 'purity of heart is to will one thing' – that what you want can only be the good (and not a reward) if it truly is to be one thing. In other words, purity of heart is the opposite of opportunism and of the *quid pro quo* or something-for-something mindset so rife in our culture. This does not mean that practising self-control is unimportant as a psychological capacity. Rather, my point is still that even though self-control – and the strength to resist temptation – is crucial to cultivating the art of missing out, it is a fairly empty and egocentric exercise if the sole aim is to obtain a greater reward. It is only endowed with meaning when employed in contexts that are existentially and ethically significant. Without these value-related dimensions, psychological thinking and practice are quickly reduced to means by which the individual can blindly satisfy their needs – i.e. to another form of pure opportunism or instrumental self-help.

Welcome to the treadmill

Another area of psychology relevant to the art of missing out is human happiness and the prevailing advice on how to achieve it. In recent years, a veritable happiness industry has sprouted up, with legions of therapists, coaches, counsellors and self-help authors promising nirvana just around the corner – if only we change the way we think, feel or act.[8] The inherent flaw in all of this is, of course, the process of individualisation mentioned above. The industry necessarily involves downplaying the significance of the individual's environment and situation, and instead claiming that 'happiness is a choice!', thus making us all personally responsible for making the right decisions if we want to be happy. Since very few (if any) of us are actually in a position simply to 'choose' to be happy, this triggers a sense of inadequacy, and an even greater need for the services provided by the happiness industry, which becomes a self-sustaining, constantly growing system. From this critical perspective, the problem is not so much that we are not always happy (which is probably just an unavoidable reality of life), but that we *think* that we should be happy all the time, and constantly chase new ideas and concepts to make us more and more happy. We may even achieve some degree of momentary happiness, but it is amazing how soon we grow accustomed to it and find ourselves again yearning for more.

The science of psychology describes this phenomenon as 'hedonic adaptation' – or, more colourfully, as the 'hedonic treadmill'. Hedonic adaptation can be defined formally and generally as adaptation to affectively relevant stimuli.[9] In other words, we get used to both the good and the bad, and they gradually cease to be considered particularly good or bad. We return to our former starting point in terms of the way in which we see the world. Our capacity to grow accustomed to certain stimuli is most likely a general feature of our physiological and psychological makeup. For example, when moving from the sunlight into a dark room, it takes time for our eyes to get used to the new level of lighting. After a while, our eyes adjust but only to the point at which we see as clearly as we did out in the light. In other words, there is a kind of baseline to which our systems have a tendency to revert after the adaptation. The word 'hedonic' comes from the Greek word for pleasure or enjoyment. Hedonic adaptation is therefore the tendency for our level of desire or happiness to return to a baseline after a change. These changes may be positive (e.g. a lottery win) or negative (e.g. a bereavement). Again, we are talking about statistical correlations, with all kinds of individual exceptions, but generally people seem to have a happiness baseline that is only temporarily altered by positive and negative changes. Some famous studies show that big lottery winners achieve only minimal gains on psychologists' happiness scales. A similar result was observed in Japan, when the wealth of its people improved five-fold during the period 1958–87, but there was no lasting impact on the subjective perception of happiness and satisfaction.[10] That is what the theory of hedonic adaptation seeks to describe.

It is, of course, perfectly acceptable to question the concept of happiness built into the theory of hedonic adaptation – it is monstrously primitive, and often quantified simply by asking the individual to rate their subjective well-being: 'On a scale of 1–10, how satisfied are you with your life at the moment?' However, studies like this probably do tell us something, and on the face of it the theory of hedonic adaptation seems to be good news. It means that if something bad happens, there is a high probability that you will soon bounce back to your previous level of subjective well-being. Unfortunately, it does have a more sinister side, too. The treadmill aspect of the concept suggests that positive experiences only produce temporary happiness, and that the only way to continue to enjoy highpoints is to keep pounding along on the treadmill. We all know the feeling. We save up for something new that we really want, spend a long time looking forward to getting it and reading reviews on the internet, and we are overjoyed when the coveted object arrives – but it does not take long before we start to lust after something new, different and better. For some people, moving from one home to another is a lifelong project, in which they never feel truly happy where they are. Others find that, more generally, the joy of conquest (of the right job or the right partner) is so short-lived that they very soon re-embark on the quest for something or someone new and better. The happiness treadmill can be never-ending, and we find ourselves running faster and faster all the time, like a drug addict constantly upping the dose just to get high.

The idea that human desires and needs are insatiable is one of the oldest insights in philosophy and the history of science. Socrates describes the problem way back in Plato's dialogue *Gorgias*:

> the part of the soul which is the seat of the desires is liable to be tossed about by words and blown up and down; and some ingenious person, probably a Sicilian or an Italian, playing with the word, invented a tale in which he called the soul a 'vessel' [. . .] and the ignorant he called the uninitiated or leaky, and the place in the souls of the uninitiated in which the desires are seated, being the intemperate and incontinent part, he compared to a vessel full of holes, because it can never be satisfied.[11]

Socrates compares human desire to a leaky bucket: no matter how much we fill it, the water leaks out again, leaving only a hole and a craving for more. At least, this is the case for the 'ignorant', as Socrates put it. For as long as philosophers have been aware of the treadmill or the leaky vessel, they have also sought to transform our relationship to our desires by means of rational thought. This applied to almost all of the ancient schools of philosophy, but the best known is probably Stoicism. The Stoics were a school of philosophy in ancient Greece and later Rome. I will not present their thinking in any great detail here (for more on Stoicism, see *Stand Firm*). Suffice to say that unlike modern happiness techniques, which usually focus on positive visualisation (imagine the fantastic things you will achieve!) and a steady expansion of human possibilities, Stoicism is more concerned with negative visualisation (imagine you lose what you have) and recognising life's inevitable limitations, with death as the ultimate horizon (*memento mori* – remember you must die – was a basic Stoic admonition). The principles of Stoicism are neatly summarised in the familiar Christian serenity prayer: 'God grant me the serenity to accept the things I cannot change, courage to change the things I can, and the wisdom to know the difference.' The point of Stoicism is that there really *are* things we cannot change, which is why it is important to learn to live with them instead of engaging in a never-ending pursuit of ways to optimise the self.

The Stoics are part of a philosophical tradition, originating in Plato and Aristotle, that values limitations rather than the absence of them. It is a perspective that might help us step off the hedonic treadmill by instilling in us an elementary gratitude for what we have, rather than whipping us ever onward into an infinite succession of new conquests once we grow accustomed to what we have. It may not imbue our lives with a constant, orgiastic happiness (such a thing is probably illusory anyway), but it may help us break with the craving for *bigger, better, more expensive, more*. At this point, it is worth noting that there are, of course, many people in the world who have a completely legitimate desire for 'more'. It is important that we avoid falling into the elitist trap I outlined earlier in the book. Of course it is fine that someone in Kenya who has spent years walking ten miles to work every day wants a bike to improve their quality of life. But perhaps it is a bit excessive for a materially rich Dane like myself to dream of owning a third racing bike, after growing accustomed to both my winter and summer racers – but I absolutely need a time-trial racer, right? From the Stoic perspective, it is not in itself invidious to have desires and dreams, but they would insist that we have a duty to consider the ethical value of those dreams. The point is not that we learn to miss out in order to prove that we have a particularly strong degree of self-control. No, the point is that we should miss out on that which poses a threat to our moral fortitude and psychological integrity, such as constantly hunting for new experiences, relationships and objects that provide a fleeting rush of happiness as we continue to plod away on the hedonic treadmill.

Defensive pessimism and positive thinking

It is a bit of a mystery why the Danes repeatedly top international rankings for happiness (again, quantified on the basis of a simple question about subjective satisfaction), but one reason may be that we have relatively low expectations of life. Presumably, the high degree of equality, welfare and interpersonal trust in Denmark has much to do with it, but perhaps low expectations do, too. This may be a little bit speculative, but a culture of *Jantelov* (Jante's Law is based on a 'who-do-you-think-you-are?' syndrome, which dictates that you should never get above yourself and that success is somewhat vulgar) and low expectations perhaps inures Danes against disappointment and failure, as we are psychologically prepared for negative outcomes. Perhaps we have engendered a form of cultural stoicism in which we like to imagine everything will go wrong so that it is easier to cope with adverse situations when they do arise. In psychological terminology, this strategy is called defensive pessimism: imagining the worst to prepare for adversity and disappointment. It is commonly thought that this strategy can reduce anxiety. One of the researchers behind the theory has even written a self-help book entitled *The Positive Power of Negative Thinking*.[12]

The title is a nod to the clergyman Norman Vincent Peale's *The Power of Positive Thinking* (1952) – perhaps the most famous self-help book in history, which has recently gained new topical relevance. Much of the worldview of the most powerful man on the planet – Donald Trump – is taken from Peale, who was attached to the Marble Collegiate Church in Manhattan, which the Trump family attended when Donald was a small boy.[13] Peale later officiated at the marriage of Trump and his first wife, and the President has often made positive comments about him ('He was the greatest guy', 'You could listen to him all day long'). Peale died in 1993, aged ninety-five, but his message lives on. His book, which has sold millions of copies, is akin to a self-help gospel and has left a lasting impression on our self-understanding – even for those of us who have not read it. The chapters bear titles like 'Believe in yourself',

'How to create your own happiness', 'How to have constant energy' and 'Inflow of new thoughts can remake you'. The basic idea – which has since been repeated in countless self-help books and self-development courses – is that by thinking positively and optimistically we can achieve almost anything. Facts are not nearly as important as our attitude to them, and that attitude must be positive. One chapter is titled 'I don't believe in defeat'. Trump has embraced this phrase and is apparently unable to imagine ever losing. For example, during the 2016 presidential election campaign, he refused to guarantee that he would accept defeat by Hillary Clinton, which reflected a catastrophic lack of faith in the democratic process and institutions – and, some would say, an equally disastrous degree of self-confidence.

With all his exaggerations and his unwavering self-belief, Trump embodies positive thinking and a seemingly insatiable desire for more power, more money, more exposure. However, his variety of positive thinking is not, of course, positive when it comes to his opponents, whom he systematically belittles and insults – it is all about him. For example, he falsely claimed that the crowd for his inauguration was huge (1.5 million, he said), and he routinely bade welcome to 'thousands of people' at his campaign rallies, when far fewer were actually present, and some of them had been paid to be there. Positive thinking has taught Trump that the mind, through positivity, can create its own reality. If you repeat 'alternative facts' often enough, reality will bend to them, and to your advantage – or, at least, you will get people to believe you. This is the exact opposite of the value of low expectations, negative visualisation and defensive pessimism. Based on the analysis in this book,

I would contend that Trump is the product of a culture that knows no bounds, which risks spawning people with no feel for the art of missing out. He is the symbol of a mentality that wants it all – and wants it now!

The tyranny of choice in a world of distractions

The psychologist Barry Schwartz is one of the leading experts on what choice means to people. His research is summarised in his book *The Paradox of Choice*.[14] The paradox lies in the fact that while greater choice in life may sound like a good thing, the negative consequences soon become apparent. Schwartz's book vividly describes the cultural landscape of invitations to consume that we now inhabit. He recounts a range of personal anecdotes about how his banal wish to buy breakfast cereal or a pair of trousers quickly accelerates into a breathless slalom through all sorts of possible choices. Many of us have tried to order a cup of coffee in a café, only to be confronted with a plethora of options, all with unfamiliar Italian names. Of course Schwartz does not deny that it can be good for people to have choices, but he presents extensive research to show that it is not always better to have more and more of them. In fact, he believes that greater choice is a contributing factor to the epidemic of depression and related disorders in the Western world. The problem, according to Schwartz, is that the modern emphasis on individualism, control and choice can deprive us of our main vaccine against depression, namely our sense of belonging to and involvement in groups and contexts. It is all too easy to end up suffering from status anxiety and working ourselves to the bone to make enough money to buy the 'right' consumer goods (i.e. those deemed desirable by contemporary culture). Of course, the depression phenomenon is a complex problem with many background factors, but perhaps the 'tyranny of choice', as Schwartz describes it, is a significant factor – especially when coupled with personal responsibility, which dictates that we have only ourselves to blame whenever we make the wrong choice. We have become accustomed to believing that life is about realising our individual preferences by breaking shackles. However, for Schwartz, the main factors that drive happiness are the close social relationships and collectives that *actually* bind us together. Happiness is not about having no ties to anyone, but about having the right ties, as I argued in *Standpoints*. Schwartz presents scientific support for this view.

I do have one bone to pick with Schwartz's book though. He takes it for granted that we live in a world of unlimited possibilities and then poses the question of how to survive it. Clearly, however, it is a false premise that we have unlimited possibilities. Nobody has that – and some people self-evidently have more options than others. Even in a relatively egalitarian society like Denmark, social and economic inequality are reproduced through social norms and the educational system. To assert that everyone has unlimited possibilities is to perpetuate an ideological construct devoid of empirical support, and serves only to blame the victims of the policies that create inequality. However, even if everyone did have access to unlimited possibilities, Schwartz is correct when he says that this would be a pretty tragic state of affairs. The very idea of a multitude of opportunities can be a destructive influence, and this seems to be backed up by the extensive scientific literature documented in his book.

Schwartz also wants to help the reader to opt out, and this is where his book is particularly relevant to the theme of missing out. He presents five recommendations:

(1) *We would be better off if we embraced certain voluntary constraints on our freedom of choice, instead of rebelling against them.* This requires consciously coming to terms with our lives. My suggestion in the next chapter is that we approach this as an aesthetic project – a life art.

(2) *We would be better off seeking that which is 'good enough' instead of seeking the best.* If we always want the best, we will almost never have reason to be satisfied. Schwartz recommends that we practise being 'satisficers' – i.e. those who are satisfied with the good enough – rather than 'maximisers', who are only satisfied with the very best. He claims that maximisers are often more susceptible to depression.

(3) *We would be better off if we lowered our expectations about the results of our decisions.* The more we experience being masters of our own destiny, the more we expect to realise our wishes. This is a vicious circle. In most cases, we have far less control over our lives than we like to think.

(4) *We would be better off if the decisions we made were non-reversible.* If that were the case, we would not constantly dwell on whether we have done the right thing.

(5) *We would be better off if we paid less attention to what others around us are doing.* This is extremely

difficult for human beings – we are notoriously social creatures and constantly compare ourselves with others.

Schwartz's basic point is that maximisation can ruin lives. He recommends that we learn to make do, to be satisfied with less than we might theoretically have had, but the ideal of almost limitless freedom of choice systematically contradicts this.

The freedom of choice presented by an enticing consumer society is one thing, the very real distractions offered by new digital technology are another. The psychologist Adam Alter of New York University has written a thought-provoking book about this.[15] He maps out the landscape of constant temptations that modern humans have to inhabit and live with. Many of us have smartphones and tablets that enable us to access an infinite amount of information – anywhere, anytime. Streaming services allow us to watch almost anything – anywhere, anytime. We have payday loans, credit cards and an advertising industry that encourages us to buy and consume – anywhere, anytime. It is all too easy to lose yourself in a Facebook feed, because they are, by design, endless. As you scroll down through a few posts, new updates are constantly being added higher up the thread. The same applies to the TV series that we now binge-watch: we have to make an active effort to turn the machine off, otherwise the next episode just starts automatically. These series are also skilfully crafted, usually culminating in a cliff-hanger to keep you hooked for just one more episode. Personally, I derive a great deal of pleasure and frustration from the computer game *Civilization*, the slogan of which is 'Just one more turn'. I find it almost impossible to stop once I have started to play.

It is precisely this combination of enjoyment and frustration that characterises the digital ecology we have created for ourselves. It is exciting and pleasurable to keep up with the content posted by our family, friends and acquaintances – as hyper-social beings, we are hardwired to be interested in this. Our favourite TV series provide a measure of aesthetic satisfaction via captivating plots and beautiful images. Most of us no longer spend our waking hours surrounded by forests and fields, but by inviting displays and applications. According to some studies, we spend more time gazing at screens than sleeping. Alter says that our digital econiche causes huge problems with addiction – addiction to the technology, the applications, the games and the series. In *Irresistible*, he emphasises the flipside of a culture that constantly invites the individual to experience and consume by clicking, scrolling, checking and watching. The problem is not just one of dependence. We also run the risk of losing important skills that we acquire by being in close physical proximity to others and paying attention to them, in particular the ability to immerse ourselves socially and to empathise. One consequence of this trend is that voluntarily detoxing from digital culture has become a desirable luxury. People who can afford it pay a lot of money to go on retreats where digital technology is banned (for example, in monasteries or hiking in the wilderness), or to send their children to elite schools where the teachers work with blackboards and chalk, not with heretical iPads. It is worth noting that the founder of Apple, Steve Jobs, allegedly refused to let his own children use the iPad that he happily sold to the rest of us.

So what is the solution? To build cultural landscapes, in our homes, schools and workplaces, with fewer of these constant invitations? Of course, we can do something about this ourselves (stop charging our smartphones beside the bed, stop using our devices late at night, turn off notifications, etc., because it is well documented that all of these disrupt our sleep). Families should reflect on the temptations of all these screens and introduce rules on the use of devices if necessary. But we also have to do something at an organisational level, both in the workplace (for example, introducing an email policy limiting the number of messages per day and when they may be sent) and in educational institutions, where we should, as a matter of urgency, do away with the fascination with digitalisation that has taken hold, where the prevailing wisdom seems to be that all learning should be imparted via tablets and laptops. Quite extensive research now suggests that the acquisition of knowledge through physical books has a clear advantage over the use of screens, which make close reading and concentration far more difficult.[16] Of course we could just sit down, practise self-control and not eat the marshmallow – but as long as we live in a landscape of temptations, this struggle is doomed to failure. We must cultivate a different landscape. And that is the subject of the next and final chapter of this book.

5

The Joy of Missing Out

The previous chapters have outlined four types of arguments – from political, existential, ethical and psychological perspectives – that exemplify and justify the art of missing out. I hope that some of these arguments have been convincing. If you have accepted their validity, learning to 'miss out' should now be politically justified, existentially important, ethically good and psychologically wise. However, not all of the arguments are necessarily especially practical or appealing. Instead, the emphasis has been on the virtue and necessity of frugality, privation and moderation (to use negative terms), and of focus, character and persistence (to use more positive terms). Some may think this sounds like a sad and grey way of life. What about pleasure and enjoyment? What about life's aesthetic dimension? This is the subject of this final chapter, in which I will argue that missing out can be a source of deep pleasure. The chapter's title, 'The Joy of Missing Out' (or JOMO), is a deliberate contrast to the desperate FOMO ('Fear of Missing Out') mentality of our day. We should not be afraid to miss out – rather, we should take pleasure in the simplicity and focus of a good human life. No matter what we do, we will always miss out on something, so the quest to do it all is something of a fool's errand. To acknowledge this is to practise JOMO instead of FOMO.

The beauty of simplicity

Generally speaking, most people understand the beauty of dropping the intricate and complex and focusing instead on the simple. After all, it is rarely the case that the more complicated a phenomenon is, the more beautiful it is. A haiku of seventeen syllables, which follows a strict template, can be just as moving as any long poem with a challenging syntax. A simple melody, sung by a beautiful voice with a simple accompaniment, can be just as moving as a complex composition. In science, it is well established that the aesthetic appeal of the simplest and most harmonious theories and evidence plays a major role. One famous example is the DNA helix, which Francis Crick, who helped discover it, called 'a molecule with style'. There is a great deal of evidence to suggest that the beautiful graphic representation of the relatively simple DNA structure was conducive to the general dissemination and appeal of the theory.

Art and science are not improved by being unnecessarily complicated, although a relatively high degree of complexity may sometimes be necessary in order to say something sufficiently precise about the topic at hand. The point is that it is the material or object itself that determines the level of complexity and the scope for precision. In mathematics, a degree of perfection and precision is achievable that is not possible in ethics or psychology, which deal with far more unstructured and complex phenomena. Aristotle argued that it is the sign of a mature intellect not to demand greater precision than the subject matter is capable of furnishing. Expressing a concept as simply and precisely as possible is the ideal, but learning to strike the right note and level is not easy, and requires a great deal of experience. In the areas of science in which I work, it is obvious that the ability to communicate simply and precisely seems to grow with experience and insight. Students writing their first assignments at university will have a tendency to write in a difficult and 'academic' style, whereas older, experienced professors have, in many cases (though not all!), found a form that is much lighter and more elegant. Conveying difficult material in a simple and understandable way is an art.

In both the arts and the sciences, an aesthetics of simplicity facilitates the precise communication of messages. Both are also fairly systematic. Although many people believe that art is by definition wild and intuitive, while only science is methodologically rigorous, there is a great deal of evidence – including from artists talking about their own practices – to suggest that art is often created methodically and systematically, and that frameworks and forms permit creativity to flow.[1] Instead of being liberating, freedom without limits is almost paralysing, because without frameworks we end up in a vacuum in which our actions elicit no response. As the Danish poet and filmmaker Jørgen Leth has put it many times, including in a conversation I had with him in 2016,[2] 'the rules of the game' are a prerequisite for artistic freedom. They provide a solid form or structure that enables the artist to make use of 'the gifts of chance' (to use Leth's expression), and in which a part of the world can be exhibited in a non-chaotic manner. In order to create beauty, the artist must restrict him- or herself. Leth expresses this philosophy in credos like 'Life is interesting. We want to study it', and 'I don't know anything. But I want to!'[3] From Leth's perspective, the artist studies the world. Art is not just a subjective outpouring of emotion, but an attempt to explore and understand the phenomena of life. In a sense, although they may go about it differently, both the artist and the scientist are trying to achieve much the same thing. Leth himself adheres to the study method pioneered by Bronislaw Malinowski, who was one of the first anthropologists to go out and live among the people he wanted to understand. Based on this approach, Leth formulated four steps for his artistic practice: find an area, delineate it, inspect it, write it down!

If this approach is valid, then the processes of selection and delimitation are prerequisites for focused artistic practice. We must choose to opt out – to miss out on most things – in order to be able to see *something*. And what applies to the arts is transferable to life in general. Just as life can be considered a scientific research project in which we study the world and learn, it can also be considered an artistic project. The French philosopher and historian Michel Foucault called this 'the aesthetics of existence',[4] by which he meant bringing back the ancient philosophical concept of the art of life, which represents a trinity of the true, the beautiful and the good. Foucault invited us to consider life as a work of art. On the one hand, this could be seen as a risky, irresponsible aestheticisation, if it is done without paying heed to our obligations to others. But on the other hand, it could be seen as a reflection of Løgstrup's 'will to form', which is intimately linked to the possibility of leading an ethical life. From this perspective, the aesthetic, correctly understood (namely as a life *art*, in which life becomes a work of art), is a prerequisite for, rather than a hindrance to, the ethical. Without an (aesthetic) form for life, it is impossible to realise our (ethical) obligations. Without restrictions, no responsibility. Without rules, no games – because in a world without limits, the strong will always get their way.

The disciplining of the will

How then do we bestow form on life? In a sense, this question lies behind all the political, existential, ethical and psychological reflections in this book. We have already become acquainted with many types of answers, but it is reasonable to sort them into two general categories. The first is about the disciplining of the will; the second concerns the relationships and contexts within which people live. We might say that the former seeks to shape life 'directly' through acts of will, the latter more 'indirectly' through our environment. Let us start by looking at the direct influences first. In the previous chapter, we encountered the psychologist Barry Schwartz, who described and problematised 'the tyranny of choice' in modern society. He says that we laud our almost boundless freedom of choice as if it were a good thing *per se*, irrespective of what the choice is *between*. This is, of course, absurd, because any rational person would prefer to choose between two good things rather than between a thousand bad ones. But, under these circumstances, how do we decide what not to choose? How do we discipline the will to help us master the art of self-restraint? In the best spirit of self-help, Schwartz offers plenty of advice on how to answer these questions. I will just present a selection, which I have allowed myself to paraphrase and expand on a little:[5]

• *Decide when to make a choice*: Don't make everything in life a situation where you have to choose. That would be mentally exhausting. In most situations, you should fall back on habit and routine. There is nothing wrong with acting in a routine manner. A life without habit and routine would be unbearable.

• *Convince yourself that the idea that 'only the best is good enough' is nonsense*: When something is good enough, it is good enough. If you are always chasing the best, happiness will elude you. In fact, the very idea of 'the best' often leads to despair, because whatever is considered best one year may be hopelessly old-fashioned the next. If only the best is good enough, then nothing is ever particularly good.

• *Make your decisions irreversible*: 'Agonizing over whether your love is "the real thing" or your sexual relationship is above or below par, and wondering whether you could have done better, is a prescription for misery', Schwartz writes.[6] A lot of decisions should not be reversed – even if we have the opportunity – especially when they involve obligations that concern our relationships with others.

• *Practise gratitude*: Easier said than done, but important nonetheless. Perhaps Kierkegaard's thoughts on the lily and the bird might serve as a source of inspiration?

Or Gelsted, with his poem about trees? There are many examples of aesthetic eulogies to the art of self-restraint.

• *Expect to be hooked*: Even the most cursory acquaintance with the concept of the hedonic treadmill discussed in the previous chapter should make you more realistic about the benefits of achieving what you want. The treadmill concept reflects the idea that we will revert to a given 'level of happiness' soon after a highly desirable event has occurred. Acknowledging this allows us to protect ourselves from disappointment when it transpires that buying a particular car or holiday home or falling in love with a new partner fails to elicit the profound and lasting sense of happiness that we expected.

• *Resist the urge to compare*: Human beings may well find it hard to resist comparing themselves with others, but being aware of this tendency may at least keep it in check. Yes, the grass always seems greener on the other side – but maybe you should mow your own lawn and play on it with the kids instead of spending time staring over the fence at the neighbour's garden. Challenge the kind of snobbery that proclaims that only certain things or ideas are good enough or worth pursuing. I can exclusively reveal that I really like the cheapest nougat ice cream from our local supermarket, and that one of the best 'meals' I have ever had was a simple focaccia from a 7-Eleven, partaken of at a bus stop one night on my way home from a party. It had the perfect combination of fat, salt and umami that my body needed right there, right then. Less really can be more!

• *Learn to live with limitations*: This, of course, is the focal point of this book. It is also the final point in Schwartz's book, and reflects his great faith in the ability of human beings to discipline themselves. However, the idea that we should use our will to practise wanting less is almost a paradox. Making do with less requires a strong will, which hints at the Achilles heel of the 'direct' method – is it really possible to 'work on yourself' and your will to such an extent that you build up enough self-control to miss out in a tempting, inviting, boundless world? A few people may be able to. Who knows, they may even benefit from self-help books on the subject. But, for most of us, an 'indirect' method will be more beneficial. In other words, an approach not focused on the will as an inner psychological phenomenon, but on the cultural landscape of institutions, systems, organisations, technologies, homes and families that surrounds us. With this in mind, we now need to discuss the form taken by these frameworks for our lives.

The creation of an aesthetic cultural landscape through rituals

How can we cultivate a landscape for human life that makes it easier to focus on what matters and miss out on what is unimportant? Again, aesthetics might help, and the aesthetics of social life are often reflected in rituals. The anthropologist Mary Douglas describes rituals as regulations for social relations that enable people to know their own community.[7] These regulations have a significant aesthetic dimension, since rituals (for example in church, at weddings or at the opening of Parliament) are often moving and remind us of the kind of society in which we live. According to Douglas, rituals sustain society. A society without them is not really a proper one – or rather, it is a society that its people find difficult to understand. Rituals endow social life with form. From this perspective, the deritualisation of modern society in recent decades, as described by numerous sociologists, is something to bemoan. Some have speculated that deritualisation liberates the individual for creative self-expression, but it is hard to imagine a freedom without ways in which to be free. Without rituals, we risk the tyranny of formlessness that Løgstrup warned against.

The sociologist Anthony Giddens describes modern society as being arranged according to 'open thresholds of experience' rather than ritualised transitions.[8] In this scenario, the influence of rituals as external points of reference is reduced – and, allegedly, we make most decisions ourselves. This applies to many of life's major transitions: birth, adolescence, marriage and death. There are, of course, still a number of rituals to mark these transitions, but many of them seem to have lost their aura of naturalness. They are increasingly charac-terised by an element of 'design', in which the individual concerned chooses whether there will be a ritual at all – and if so, what form it will take. This is seen most clearly, perhaps, in rites of passage from childhood to adolescence and adulthood (confirmation, bar mitzvah and so on), but also in marriage and childbirth (see, for example, the concept of 'designer births'). The indi-vidual has become a consumer who is expected to piece together a life from the available menus. As a result, not much is taken for granted any more (or treated ritu-ally). Most aspects of life can be reconsidered, chosen or not chosen. As an extension of this, Giddens considers whether the relative absence of rituals in contemporary social contexts removes an important psychological foundation for the individual's ability to cope with these transitions. He writes that the traditional rites of passage brought 'those concerned into touch with wider cosmic forces, relating individual life to more encompassing existential issues'.[9]

The deritualisation of the social represents a weakening of the bond between individuals and the greater moral framework for life – often in the name of individualisation and authenticity. However, this is a risky strategy, because all societies need rituals so that people can spend time together in civilised ways. Rituals enable us to interact with each other in a fruitful manner. It is not inauthentic or dishonest to act in the public space on the basis of certain ritualised templates. The philosopher Anthony Holiday builds on Douglas when he argues that respect for rituals is a universal moral value.[10] Of course, this is not to suggest that every ritual has moral value. Rather, it means that in a society without some degree of ritualisation, morality is not possible. According to Holiday, we can only maintain moral integrity if we accept and respect certain rituals – including the right to freedom of speech and assembly (civil rights). Holiday, who died in 2006, knew what he was talking about. As a South African, he had devoted much of his life to fighting the apartheid regime's arbitrary exercise of power, and spent six years in prison before going into exile in England. He was inspired by the Austrian philosopher Ludwig Wittgenstein's philosophy of language, according to which language must be understood as what he called 'a form of life'. Holiday believed that a cultivated linguistic form of life is only possible if we assume that some universal moral values apply, including truth, justice and respect for rituals. Based on Holiday's analysis, it would not be possible to have morals without rituals, because rituals are a prerequisite for linguistic community. Again, we see that the aesthetic form of life – including on a collective level – is intimately linked to the possibility of establishing ethical forms of life.

We must, therefore, seek to create a cultural ecology with aesthetically appealing rituals that allow for an ethically based form of life. These are found to varying degrees in all cultures – for example, the Japanese tea ceremony, or singing happy birthday and blowing out the candles on a birthday cake – and are used to focus collective attention on important matters in certain situations. Every individual can seek to cultivate their own small landscape of everyday rituals to endow their lives with form, but this also has to be done at the collective level, where people do things together (especially in workplaces and educational institutions). Thinking in terms of aesthetic landscapes and environments (rather than purely in terms of inner will-power) can also serve as a counterweight to the risk of dependence on various technologies, as discussed in the previous chapter. Sometimes psychology does not need to be particularly difficult, for example when it comes to habits and will-power. As Adam Alter points out in his book *Irresistible*, it is little wonder we submit to temptation if we surround ourselves with it – conversely, it is much easier to find will-power if we remove temptations from our surroundings. The point is to cultivate a landscape – and this is also a precondition for putting down roots, to return to the basic metaphor in *Stand Firm*. Without landscapes in which to sink roots, rootlessness is hard to avoid. Simone Weil – the French philosopher, anarchist and mystic, whose works included *The Need for Roots*, and who died young of tuberculosis and starvation during the Second World War – thought that putting down roots is the most important yet least recognised human need.[11] Many of our problems stem not only from a lack of roots, but from a lack of understanding of their importance. It is partly through rituals that we discover the value of being rooted. But how do we do this? I will conclude by outlining some more or less practical proposals to complement the more individual and will-power-based advice outlined so far:

• As a society, we should recognise that knowledge of the past and acknowledgement of cultural traditions do not preclude the individual's freedom of self-expression. Our schools and education system should not be afraid to reconstruct and reproduce the experiences of the past. Understanding society's roots is not reactionary, but a prerequisite for acknowledging that life is lived in communities. These days, many people seek hope in innovation and disruption, but if such practices stand on their own, life has no form or limits. To be able to think innovatively in a practical way, we must first know how our time and place fits into the historical perspective. We might express this by saying that the contemporary ideal of the flexible, innovative, proactive and self-managing person, who is always willing to change, generates an in-built reluctance to 'miss out'.[12] I recently read an article by a futurologist from the consultancy Dare Disrupt, in which the author outlined the types of people that will be in demand in the society of the future, for which we need to 'educate ourselves throughout our lives'.[13] He predicted that we will need to be coders, creatives, managers, carers, entrepreneurs and artists. Aside, perhaps, from the carer, all of these are creative, innovative and disruptive roles based on breaking boundaries, initiating, renewing and self-development. Less attention is paid to the need for social maintenance and repetition. The ideal is the identity artist who constantly reinvents him- or herself, who is an entrepreneur of his or her own life, always launching the next existential start-up. As soon as one project is ready to fly, it is left behind, and a new and different one taken up.

There may be a few people who approximate this ideal, but for many of us it is problematic. Nevertheless, we are forced to try to live up to it at appraisal interviews, on personal development courses, or by other types of development practices. We often fail and end up stressed and mentally exhausted – or, frustrated by our impotence, we begin to play bullshit bingo, regurgitating the empty buzzwords used by managers, coaches or consultants when they talk up the demand for innovation and disruption.[14]

If we return to our earlier metaphor drawn from the art world, we can say that the artist is and should remain an exception. If we were all disruptive artists all the time, nothing in society would be coherent. No one would be obliged to do anything other than follow whatever short-term whims took their fancy. Fortunately, many people are instead curators, those who set up permanent exhibitions based on unifying themes and help to rein in the unruly artists. Despite the widespread academic-bashing, this may be their legitimate function – to produce fair and equitable systems with a degree of stability that make a society transparent to its people. Even better, some act as custodians, maintaining and protecting what already exists. Custodians help to preserve what is important from the threat posed by the emphasis on short-term disruption. We should thank them for that. The curators and custodians of life – the maintainers, as some have started calling them – should be in demand in job advertisements and well remunerated for their efforts. They should not be ashamed that they are not artists or entrepreneurs – quite the contrary, because artistic innovation is, in fact, only possible when there are others who are curators and custodians, creating frameworks and maintaining them, rather than always pushing the boundaries and breaking things down. Being a custodian is in itself a life art, and there will be a great need for them in the future.

• Extending the idea of resurrecting the custodian as a legitimate existential figure, society as a whole should also focus on ethical upbringing. Getting used to missing out presupposes an ethical maturity that should be nurtured in both families and schools. In educational contexts, we have long coveted skills development and self-optimisation, with a focus on everything that the PISA studies and national tests quantify. However, the school system's most important job should be to form responsible citizens who are capable of preserving and renewing democracy. For far too long, schools have operated in a manner that meets the competition state's demand for 'opportunists' who score highly in various tests – we need to shift the emphasis back to ethics and democracy. We must teach the citizens of the future to do what is right because it is right, and not because they stand to gain from it. We need to reward them for sharing their marshmallows rather than hoarding them. We must understand that this kind of upbringing is the opposite of opportunism; that it is based on respect for the virtues of moderation and self-restraint that are essential for our ability to cope with the crises described at the start of this book.

It should be noted that this kind of ethical learning is in no way a challenge to academic learning. On the contrary, it is based on the insight that the world is much bigger than the individual – a point that can be communicated through a range of disciplines, from history to mathematics.

• More broadly, we should also recognise the role of chance in human life. The idea that everyone is the master of their own destiny, and that 'we can be whatever we want' if only we are sufficiently motivated, is problematic because it is based on a philosophy of never-ending development and optimisation, and because it leads to an individualistic diagnosis which says that we only have ourselves to blame if things go awry. In recent years, a lot of social systems have been making the individual responsible for all sorts of things over which they do not necessarily have control, such as unemployment, poverty, disease and social problems – irrespective of whether such problems are actually caused by changes in political systems or economic trends. However, by designing systems that are based to a greater extent on the idea that no individual is master of their own destiny, we can encourage greater solidarity. This might even increase the willingness of the most well-off to accept less, because one day they might fall victim to chance or illness and find themselves vulnerable and in need of help. We must learn to 'miss out' not as an empty exercise in asceticism, but to ensure that there is enough for everyone. I live in Denmark, which is both a highly egalitarian society and (according to international rankings) a very happy one. We should acknowledge that the relatively small difference between top and bottom, rich and poor, is a significant reason why the country is considered one of the most harmonious and successful in the world.[15] Equality is not an end in itself, but it has proven to be a precious commodity in a world where global inequality is increasingly spiralling out of control.

• In slightly abstract terms, it would also be a good idea to reflect on a more cyclical view of time. The boundless *more, more, more* thinking, which dictates that we should not miss out on anything, is associated with a linear view. We are encouraged to continue to grow throughout our lives, as part of a lifelong learning process. The consequence of this is a requirement for eternal optimisation – in other words, we need to do more next year than this year. Many of us are trapped on both the hamster wheel and the hedonic treadmill, the results of which are clear to see in the statistics for stress, depression and anxiety. In times gone by, we had more of an understanding that life is interwoven into larger contexts that involve ups and downs. We knew that 'everything has its time', as it says in Ecclesiastes. We should probably again acknowledge that life is not just determined by the individual's inner motivation, but also by external elements, e.g. seasonal and cyclical changes. The experienced custodian knows that what is fashionable one year may be outmoded the next, and that something old will soon be back in style again. We should not be afraid of repetition – as Kierkegaard stated, it is repetition that bestows form on both our individual and collective lives. Without cyclic repetition, life dissolves into an 'empty noise devoid of content', as he wrote in *Repetition*.[16] Without repetition, there is no obligation. Repetition is getting up every morning and making packed lunches for the kids. Repetition is visiting old friends, even when they are depressed and not a great deal of fun. In reality, this entails a form of courage – the courage to do the same as usual, because it is the right thing to do. As this book asserts, it also requires that we opt out – including from potentially exciting new relationships. If we want to be friends with everyone, we cannot truly have a friend. If we want to do something well, we cannot do it all.

Throughout this book, I have advocated the art of self-restraint as a virtue, and attempted to show how a culture that knows no limits is not fertile ground for it. In conclusion, I have tried to distinguish between ways of showing restraint and opting out based on the individual's own will (the direct method), as well as ways that more indirectly cultivate the landscapes that bestow form on people's lives. The philosopher Matthew Crawford speaks of the necessity of working together to create 'ecologies of attention' if we want to escape the constant distractions and insatiable needs created by the boundless self-development culture.[17] This can be done at the individual level (in terms of how we organise our own lives), at the organisational level (in our workplaces) and at the societal level (in relation to our schools, social systems, hospitals and pensions). In general, the landscape metaphor is quite apposite. It is not simply a matter of having the will-power to step off the treadmill, it is also about creating a culture in which the treadmill does not even exist. My theory that this is best achieved through rituals and aesthetics is embryonic at best, and will require considerable further discussion to flesh it out. Nonetheless, I think that a collective shaping of our lives can curb the boundless culture that has continued to accelerate over the last half-century, resulting in the rapid spread of symptoms such as stress and unrestrained self-realisation.

I hope that the ideas contained in this book will inspire others to engage in constructive debates about missing out, and to respect the concept of moderation in general. I hope the book will be seen as a counter-balance to all forms of extremism. Those fond of a good paradox might even call it *extremely moderate*.

Notes

Introduction: Having It All

1 See Harry Wolcott, *Writing Up Qualitative Research*, 3rd edn, Sage, 2009.

1 The Sustainable Society

1 As analysed in my book *Stand Firm: Resisting the Self-Improvement Craze*, Polity, 2017.
2 Ove Kaj Pedersen, *Konkurrencestaten* (The Competitive State), Hans Reitzel, 2011.
3 Jørgen Steen Nielsen, 'Velkommen til antropocæn' (Welcome to the Anthropocene Epoch), *Information*, 27 June 2011, https://www.information.dk/udland/2011/06/velkommen-antropocaen.
4 Elizabeth Kolbert, *The Sixth Extinction: An Unnatural History*, Bloomsbury, 2014. Arne Johan Vetlesen and Rasmus Willig summarise many of the most alarming problems in their upcoming book *Hvad skal vi svare?* (What's the Answer?). I would like to thank the authors for allowing me to read it in advance of publication.
5 See this article, for example: https://www.theguardian.

com/environment/2018/apr/26/were-doomed-mayer-hill
man-on-the-climate-reality-no-one-else-will-dare-mention.

6 Jason Hickel, *The Divide: A Brief Guide to Global Inequality and its Solutions*, William Heinesen, 2017.

7 Richard Wilkinson and Kate Pickett, *The Spirit Level: Why Equality is Better for Everyone*, Penguin, 2009.

8 See http://www.oecd.org/social/inequality.htm.

9 Paul Mason, *Postcapitalism: A Guide to Our Future*, Penguin, 2016.

10 Ibid.

11 Hartmut Rosa, *Social Acceleration: A New Theory of Modernity*, Columbia University Press, 2015.

12 Zygmunt Bauman, *Liquid Modernity*, Polity, 2000.

13 I covered this in *Stand Firm*.

14 See Anders Petersen, *Præstationssamfundet* (The Performance Society), Hans Reitzel, 2016.

15 For example, in his classic *Risk Society*, Sage, 1992.

16 Robert Goodin, *On Settling*, Princeton University Press, 2012.

17 Among its defenders was the seventeenth-century legal philosopher Hugo Grotius.

18 Benjamin Barber, *Consumed: How Markets Corrupt Children, Infantilize Adults, and Swallow Citizens Whole*, Norton, 2007.

19 Other concepts seem to have supplanted 'simple living', e.g. the 'slow living' movement, which can be seen as a resistance to the social acceleration identified by Hartmut Rosa and others.

20 Jerome Segal, *Graceful Simplicity: The Philosophy and Politics of the Alternative American Dream*, University of California Press, 2006.

21 See https://yougov.co.uk/news/2015/08/12/british-jobs-meaningless.

22 See http://evonomics.com/why-capitalism-creates-point less-jobs-david-graeber.

23 This was the theme of my book *Standpoints: 10 Old Ideas in a New World*, Polity, 2018.

2 Pursuing the Good

1 The idea of finiteness as an existential condition for human values is covered in *Standpoints*.
2 Knud Ejler Løgstrup, *Den etiske fordring* (The Ethical Demand), Gyldendal, 1956, p. 19.
3 Sennett writes about this in *The Fall of Public Man*, Penguin, 1977.
4 See http://www.naturalthinker.net/trl/texts/Kierkegaard, Soren/PurityofHeart/showchapter4.html.
5 Ibid.
6 Søren Kierkegaard, *Upbuilding Discourses in Various Spirits*, edited and translated by Howard V. Hong and Edna H. Hong, Princeton University Press, 2009, p. 38.
7 Ibid., p. 39.
8 This was a major theme in my book *Standpoints*.
9 Kierkegaard, *Upbuilding Discourses in Various Spirits*, pp. 51–2.
10 H. Gollwitzer, K. Kuhn and R. Schneider (eds), *Dying We Live*, Fontana, 1976.
11 I also analysed this in *Standpoints*.
12 Published in the essay collection of the same name: Harry G. Frankfurt, *The Importance of What We Care About*, Cambridge University Press, 1998.
13 Lise Gormsen, 'Doktor, hvordan skal jeg leve mit liv?', in C. Eriksen (ed.), *Det meningsfulde liv*, Aarhus Universitetsforlag, 2003.
14 In this book, I use the words *ethics* and *morality* synonymously. The former is Greek, the latter Latin. In the original meaning of ethical, caring for roses in the garden would actually have ethical significance, as the term refers

to the entire form a life takes. Aristotle would probably have used the term in that way, but today the concepts of ethics and morality are narrower, with no consensus on the distinction between them.

15 Frankfurt, *The Importance of What We Care About*, p. 89.
16 Adam Phillips, *Missing Out: In Praise of the Unlived Life*, Farrar, Straus & Giroux, 2012.
17 Ibid., p. xv.
18 Max Weber, *The Protestant Ethic and the Spirit of Capitalism*, George Allen & Unwin, 1930.

3 The Value of Moderation

1 See Chapter 2, note 14, for discussion of the terms 'ethical' and 'moral'.
2 One classic article is Daniel Kahneman, Jack L. Knetsch and Richard H. Thaler, 'Fairness and the Assumptions of Economics', *Journal of Business* 59 (1986), S285–S300.
3 The results of Engel's study are available at: https://www.coll.mpg.de/pdf_dat/2010_07online.pdf.
4 Donald Winnicott, 'The Theory of the Parent-Infant Relationship', *International Journal of Psychoanalysis* 41 (1960), 585–95.
5 The concept of passive nihilism is taken from the philosopher Simon Critchley. See his book *Infinitely Demanding: Ethics of Commitment, Politics of Resistance*, Verso, 2007.
6 The following is based on Søren Kierkegaard, *Lilien paa Marken og Fuglen under Himlen: Tre gudelige Taler* (The Lily of the Field and the Bird of the Air: Three Devotional Speeches), 1849.
7 Ibid.
8 Karl Ove Knausgård, *Spring*, translated by Ingvild Burkey, Harvill Secker, 2018.

9 Kierkegaard, *Lilien paa Marken og Fuglen under Himlen*.
10 I would also refer to Anne-Marie Christensen's excellent book *Moderne dydsetik – arven fra Aristoteles* (Modern Virtue Ethics – the Legacy of Aristotle), Aarhus University Press, 2008.
11 Harry Clor, *On Moderation: Defending an Ancient Virtue in a Modern World*, Baylor University Press, 2008.
12 Ibid., p. 10. Since Clor wrote those words, his country has elected Donald Trump as president, and no matter what you might think about that, it is clear that Trump represents the exact opposite, i.e. confrontational and inflammatory rhetoric ('lock her up!').
13 Paul Ricoeur, *Oneself as Another*, University of Chicago Press, 1992.
14 I analysed this in my book *Identitet: Udfordringer i for-brugersamfundet* (Identity: Challenges in the Consumer Society), Klim, 2008.
15 Kenneth Gergen, *Realities and Relationships*, Harvard University Press, 1994, p. 249.
16 Goodin, *On Settling*, p. 64.

4 Marshmallows and Treadmills

1 Walter Mischel, *The Marshmallow Test: Understanding Self-control and How to Master It*, Transworld Publishers, 2015.
2 The experiment and its reception history are scrutinised in Ole Jacob Madsen, *'Det er innover vi må gå'. En kulturpsykologisk studie av selvhjelp* ('We Must Turn Inwards': A Cultural Psychological Study of Self-help), Universitetsforlaget, 2014.
3 Alan Buckingham, 'Doing Better, Feeling Scared: Health Statistics and the Culture of Fear'. In D. Wainwright (ed.), *A Sociology of Health*, Sage, 2008.
4 Celeste Kidd et al., 'Rational Snacking: Young Children's

Decision-making on the Marshmallow Task is Moderated by Beliefs About Environmental Reliability', *Cognition* 126:1 (2013), 109–14. A more detailed discussion can be found in Madsen, *'Det er innover vi må gå'. En kultur-psykologisk studie av selvhjelp.*

5 This was one of the main points in my book *Stand Firm*, which criticised the tendency to individualise whatever problems people might have and subject them to a psychological perspective.
6 I argued words to this effect in the book *Standpoints*.
7 Pedersen, *Konkurrencestaten*, p. 190.
8 William Davies, *The Happiness Industry: How the Government and Big Business Sold Us Well-Being*, Verso, 2015.
9 Shane Frederick and George Loewenstein, 'Hedonic Adaptation'. In D. Kahneman, E. Diener and N. Schwarz (eds), *Well-Being: The Foundations of Hedonic Psychology*, Russell Sage Foundation, 1999, p. 302.
10 Ibid., p. 313.
11 Quoted from http://www.gutenberg.org/files/1672/1672-h/1672-h.htm.
12 Julie Norem, *The Positive Power of Negative Thinking*, Basic Books, 2001.
13 The following was printed in a different form in an opinion piece in the newspaper *Politiken*: http://politiken.dk/debat/debatindlaeg/art5856925/Det-er-den-positive-t%C3%A6nkning-der-har-l%C3%A6rt-Trump-at-han-bare-kan-skabe-sin-egen-virkelighed.
14 Barry Schwartz, *The Paradox of Choice: Why More is Less*, HarperCollins, 2004.
15 Adam Alter, *Irresistible: Why We Can't Stop Checking, Scrolling, Clicking and Watching*, The Bodley Head, 2017. The following recycles passages from a piece I wrote in *Politiken*: http://politiken.dk/kultur/art5935742/

Mindst-hvert-femte-minut-m%C3%A6rker-jeg-en-trang
-til-at-tjekke-min-smartphone.
16 See Naomi S. Baron, *Words Onscreen: The Fate of
Reading in a Digital World*, Oxford University Press,
2015.

5 The Joy of Missing Out

1 This has been a major theme in my colleague Lene
Tanggaard's work on creativity, which I find most inspir-
ing.
2 In the Rosenkjær series *Det meningsfulde liv* (The
Meaningful Life), first broadcast on 27 September 2016.
3 See, e.g., Jørgen Leth, 'Tilfældets gifts: En filmisk poetik'
(The Gifts of Chance: A Cinematic Poetry), *Kritik* (2006),
2–10; and Jonathan Wichmann, *Leth og kedsomheden*
(Leth and Boredom), Information Publishing, 2007.
4 Michel Foucault, 'On the Genealogy of Ethics: An
Overview of Work in Progress'. In Paul Rabinow (ed.),
The Foucault Reader, Penguin, 1984.
5 Schwartz, *The Paradox of Choice*.
6 Ibid, p. 229.
7 Mary Douglas, *Purity and Danger*, Routledge & Kegan
Paul, 1966, p. 128.
8 Anthony Giddens, *Modernity and Self-identity: Self and
Society in the Late Modern Age*, Polity Press, 1991. See
also my analysis of his work in my 2008 book *Identitet:
Udfordringer i forbrugersamfundet*, from which some of
these passages are taken.
9 Giddens, *Modernity and Self-identity*, p. 204.
10 Anthony Holiday, *Moral Powers: Normative Necessity in
Language and History*, Routledge, 1988.
11 Simone Weil, *The Need for Roots*, Routledge, 2002
(originally published 1949).
12 The following is based on an opinion piece originally

published in *Politiken*: http://politiken.dk/kultur/art597
3426/Nej-tak-Hella-Joof-hvorfor-i-alverden-skal-vi-disrup
te-vores-liv.

13 See http://politiken.dk/indland/uddannelse/studieliv/art59
61892/Fremtidens-seks-typer-%E2%80%93-som-vi-skal-
uddanne-os-til-hele-livet.

14 Bullshit bingo is a parody in which instead of numbers,
you tick off some of today's empty clichés and buzzwords
('disruption', 'innovation', etc.). When a middle manager
or consultant uses these words, you cross them off one
at a time, and shout 'House!' when your card is full.
The purpose of the game is to deconstruct cliché-ridden
presentations.

15 See Wilkinson and Pickett, *The Spirit Level: Why Equality
is Better for Everyone*.

16 See Søren Kierkegaard, *Fear and Trembling* and
Repetition, edited and translated by Howard V. Hong
and Edna H. Hong, Princeton University Press, 1983.

17 Matthew B. Crawford, *The World Beyond Your Head:
On Becoming an Individual in an Age of Distraction*,
Farrar, Straus and Giroux, 2015.

'*The Joy of Missing Out* makes a powerful, compelling and much-needed argument for self-restraint – on pragmatic grounds, moral grounds, psychological grounds and even aesthetic grounds. Be sure to read this book before your next shopping trip, or job change, or relationship change. This is as good a case as I have seen for when and why less can be more.'

BARRY SCHWARTZ, AUTHOR OF *THE PARADOX OF CHOICE* AND CO-AUTHOR OF *PRACTICAL WISDOM*

'Because you're worth it', proclaims the classic cosmetics ad. 'Just do it!' implores the global sports retailer. Everywhere we turn, we are constantly encouraged to experience as much as possible, for as long as possible, in as many ways as possible. FOMO – Fear of Missing Out – has become a central preoccupation in a world fixated on the never-ending pursuit of gratification and self-fulfilment.

But this pursuit can become a treadmill leading nowhere. How can we break out of it? In this refreshing book, bestselling Danish philosopher and psychologist Svend Brinkmann reveals the many virtues of missing out on the constant choices and temptations that dominate our experience-obsessed consumer society. By cultivating self-restraint and celebrating moderation we can develop a more fulfilling way of living that enriches ourselves and our fellow humans and protects the planet we all share – in short, we can discover the joy of missing out.

COVER DESIGN AND ILLUSTRATION BY DAVID A. GEE
PRINTED IN THE UNITED STATES

polity

POLITYBOOKS.COM

9 781509 531578 >